THE FORMATIVE PERIOD IN ALABAMA,
1815-1828

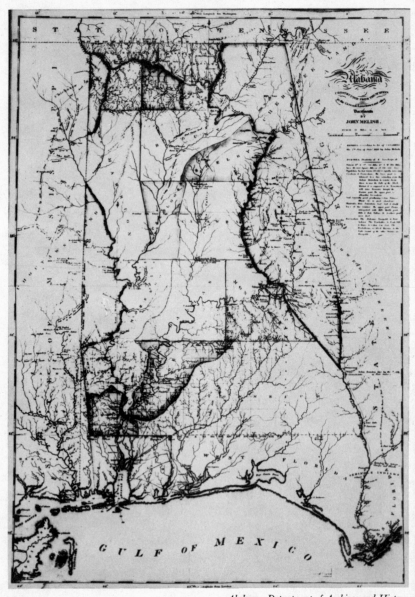

Alabama Department of Archives and History

SOUTHERN HISTORICAL PUBLICATIONS
No. 8

The Formative Period in Alabama, 1815-1828

BY

Thomas Perkins Abernethy

*Emeritus Professor of History,
University of Virginia*

UNIVERSITY OF ALABAMA PRESS
University, Alabama

F
326
. A14
1965

Contents

List of Maps and Charts

Preface

DR. A. C. COLE BEGINS HIS STUDY OF *The Whig Party in the South* with the year 1830, but necessarily, the basis for the confusing political alignments of the Southern Whigs lay largely in the years that had gone before the actual formation of the party. Alabama received her first great influx of population and underwent the formative period of her development during the apparently quiet administration of Monroe, when party lines were not recognized as existing. The new conditions of the frontier are sure to change old habits and old views, but the absolute lack of avowed partisan division during the period when Alabama was receiving her first wave of population gives us an especially good chance to study a society where men's political views are almost certain to be based directly on economic interest or individual conviction. With this in mind, it has been with the double purpose of obtaining an understanding of the conditions under which the cotton kingdom was planted on the Gulf Coast, and of trying to discover the process by which fixed party principles were crystallized out of the solution of social and economic elements which existed in Alabama during the period of settlement following the War of 1812, that the present work was undertaken.

Substantial source material, principally in the Library of Congress, the Public Library of New York City, the Alabama Department of Archives and History, the Mississippi Department

9

of Archives and History, and the Young Men's Christian Association Library of Mobile, has been searched, but there are important gaps in the body of information collected. This is especially the case in connection with the subjects of agriculture and slave-management, but, as the discovery of local peculiarities was the principal object of the study, it has seemed best not to fill in these blanks from general accounts. Only such information as deals particularly with Alabama has been used.

In connection with questions of politics, there also has been difficulty. In a period of settlement and of political uncertainty, there are few established lines of policy to guide the student on his way. But, on the other hand, there is added interest in discovering from among the various problems which confront the community, the ones which develop sufficient significance to shape the course of events and to become solidified into partisan principles. Thus the study of the formative period has afforded an opportunity to find the principal questions upon which the people were divided, and hence to gain some understanding of the basis of later alignments. But, even so, many points upon which we would like to have information are left in comparative and tantalizing obscurity. The principal cause for this, as it appears to the writer, is that the questions which agitated the men of these early years were largely local matters, and the political leaders had not yet gained sufficient importance outside their own state to enable them to make a lasting impression. One of the politicians who grew up with Alabama was William R. King, but, though he was later elected Vice-President of the United States, we have few records to reveal his mind during the interesting time when his career was taking shape. And so it is for most of the others.

This work, submitted as a doctoral dissertation to the Faculty of the Graduate School of Arts and Sciences of Harvard University, was prepared under the stimulating direction of Professor Frederick Jackson Turner. The materials collected by the late Dr. Thomas M. Owen, of the Alabama State Department of Archives and History, made the research possible. Each of these men has been of inestimable aid and encouragement in my work.

I am indebted also to Dr. Dunbar Rowland, of the Mississippi State Department of Archives and History, and to Mr. J. C. Fitzpatrick, of the Manuscript Division of the Library of Congress, for aid in the collection of materials. Professor L. C. Gray, of the United States Department of Agriculture, Office of Farm Management, kindly read the chapter dealing with agriculture; and Dr. Roland M. Harper, of the Alabama Geological Survey, gave me valuable aid in connection with geographical questions, but of course the writer is responsible for the treatment of these subjects given herein.

THOMAS P. ABERNETHY

Preface to the Second Edition

IT IS PLEASANT, AFTER AN INTERVAL OF FORTY-two years, to come again to the modest project which was my first effort to become a historian. I am grateful to Ernest A. Seemann, director of the University of Alabama Press, for proposing to bring out a new and improved edition, and to my wife, Ida Robertson Abernethy, for doing, as always, the lion's share of the editorial work. It has been our object to amend, rather than to change, the presentation of the subject. Since the treatment of the material was intended to be purely factual, no alteration of interpretation was called for, and since we had no intention of writing a new book, no extensive elaboration seemed desirable. We have tried only to make detailed improvements on the original edition, and in this we hope we have succeeded. Awkward sentences have been made smooth; much unnecessary punctuation has been eliminated; many unnecessary words have been deleted. A little repetitious material has been omitted, and in a few instances the original text has been changed to conform with new findings. The original maps and charts have been redrawn and placed with the chapters to which they apply. We hope this small contribution throws some significant light upon a crucial phase of Alabama's history.

THOMAS PERKINS ABERNETHY

University of Virginia
September, 1965

THE FORMATIVE PERIOD IN ALABAMA, 1815-1828

CHAPTER ONE

The Mississippi Territory

WHEN ENGLAND RECEIVED WEST FLORIDA FROM
Spain at the close of the Seven Years' War, its northern boundary was the thirty-first parallel; but England later, for administrative purposes, changed the line so that it ran from the Chattahoochee due westward along the parallel of thirty-two degrees,
twenty-eight minutes, to the point where the Yazoo flows into
the Mississippi. When Spain recovered the Floridas at the close
of the American Revolution, she insisted on the northern boundary as fixed by England, but the United States protested, and
finally won the point when the treaty of 1795 fixed the thirty-
first parallel as the international boundary.

The disputed territory, which extended from the Mississippi
to the Chattahoochee, was finally evacuated by Spain in 1798,
and the next year, the United States, with the acquiescence of
Georgia, which also laid claim to the land, established a territorial form of government for the district.[1] This was the original
Mississippi Territory. In 1800 an elective assembly was author-
ized,[2] and in 1802 Georgia relinquished her claim.[3] After two
more years, the boundary was extended northward to the Tennessee line,[4] and thus the Territory came to include all that land
which is embraced by the present states of Alabama and Mississippi, except that which lies below the thirty-first degree of
latitude.

Within this extensive area there were but two white settle-

17

ments: one upon the lower Mississippi, and the other upon the lower Tombigbee River. Those who lived upon the Tombigbee had filtered through the Indian country from the time of the Revolution onward; some were Tory refugees, some were patriots who had left their old homes to seek new ones, and some were traders with the Indians. The blood of these men was various: English and Scottish traders mingled with Yankee frontiersmen, and many of them had taken native wives. The half-breeds were often men of wealth, and no distinction of race seems to have been made in the rugged life of the frontier.[5]

St. Stephens, a primitive village of log cabins, was the principal settlement in the Tombigbee region, and here the government established a post for trading with the Choctaw Indians and, as soon as Georgia gave up her claim to the soil, a land office. The act arranging for the disposal of the public domain was passed in 1803.[6] It provided for the validation of claims under British and Spanish grants, quieted claims under the act of Georgia establishing Bourbon County in 1785,[7] granted tracts of 640 acres to actual settlers at the time of the Spanish evacuation, and gave preëmption rights to settlers occupying land at the time the act was passed. Settling on public lands was forbidden, but squatters continued to come in, and an act of 1807 extended preëmption rights to those who had already come, but once more prohibited entries upon government lands for the future. Lands not otherwise appropriated were to be surveyed and put on sale at public auction according to the provisions which had already been adopted for the Northwest Territory. Consequently in 1807 the first sales took place at St. Stephens.[8]

In 1806 the government acquired from the Indians a small triangle of land lying between the Tennessee border and the great bend in the Tennessee River. In 1809 this tract, the original Madison County, was offered for sale and readily taken up by cotton planters from Georgia. Here Huntsville was built around a great spring and soon came to be the commercial center of the new region.[9]

Cotton was raised in the Alabama-Tombigbee region as early

as 1772;[10] the manufacture of cotton cloth was begun by the Cherokees in 1796-97;[11] and Colonel Benjamin Hawkins, who was for many years agent for the Creeks, states in his A Sketch of the Creek Country, 1798-1799 that a Scottish trader, who had made his home among the Indians and had taken a native woman for his wife, first raised a quantity of green seed cotton for the market, but, finding it more profitable to manufacture his own staple, employed eleven hands, besides his own family, in the industry.[12] In 1802 the first cotton gins were introduced into the Alabama country, two of the three of them being set up among the Indians.[13] By 1808 the staple had come to be the leading agricultural product of the region.[14]

From the very first its culture among the whites seems to have been associated with Negro labor, for in 1810 slaves made up nearly 40 percent of the population upon the lower Tombigbee; and ten years later, after the cotton régime was well begun, the proportion of slaves in this early-settled region remained abnormally high. The men who entered Madison County in 1809 were largely Georgia planters of considerable means. They came especially for the purpose of raising cotton, and their slaves were numerous. Their entrance into the Mississippi Territory at this time indicates that the cotton régime might have begun earlier had not the War of 1812 intervened to delay it.

But the culture of cotton was still in its infancy in 1812. Scrawny hogs, whose ancestors are supposed to have been left by DeSoto and whose descendants are said to be the modern razor-back, roamed the woods; and in the canebrake region near the Gulf, large herds of cattle, sometimes numbering many hundreds, found their own forage, summer and winter alike.

Aside from the fur trade with the natives and the growing cotton industry, there seems to have been little commerce carried on during these years in the Alabama country, and the reason is not difficult to find. Mobile, the only accessible outlet, was in the hands of the Spanish, and the duties they charged were almost prohibitive. In order to avoid the payment of them, Colonel Strother Gaines, the agent at St. Stephens for the Choctaws, brought his supplies down the Tennessee River to Colbert's Ferry, above Muscle Shoals, carried them over a portage, which came to be known as Gaines' Trace, to the head of navigation on the Tombigbee at Cotton Gin Port; and thence floated them down to St. Stephens.[15] This was the route by which a number of the early Tombigbee settlers reached their destination,[16] and it long remained an important route of travel for the pioneer.

Until 1806, rivers and Indian trails were the only means of communication in the Alabama region, but in that year Congress provided for the construction of the first two roads.[17] One was to connect Nashville, Tennessee, with Natchez upon the Mississippi, crossing the Tennessee River at Muscle Shoals. It was known as the Natchez Trace and came to be a highway of no little importance in the western country. The other was to follow the route from Athens, Georgia, to New Orleans, passing through the settlement on the Tombigbee. It came to be known as the Federal Road, and along it thousands of settlers later found their way to Alabama.

Such were the slender bands of communication which tied the frontier settlements of the eastern Mississippi Territory to the world from which they were separated by hundreds of miles of Indian wilderness. Between the Tombigbee clearings and the settled part of Georgia lay the confederacy of the Creeks, extending its boundaries northward well toward the Tennessee line. Adjoining the Creeks on the north lay the territory of the Cherokees, stretching eastward into Georgia and northward into Tennessee. Between the Tombigbee and the settlements upon the lower Mississippi lay the lands of the Choctaws, and northward of them the country of the Chickasaws took in the northwestern corner of the future Alabama and extended across western Tennessee.

These Indian tribes of the South were further advanced toward civilization than were most of their North American kinsmen, and, though the westward migration of the whites was still in its infancy, they saw clearly the problem which confronted them. They had two alternatives compatible with peace: to perfect themselves in the arts of civilization, so as to compete with the newcomers, or to be driven off the land which had been theirs for untold generations. There was but one other possibility—to fight.

Already game had become too scarce to be relied upon as the only source of food supply,[18] and all the southern Indians engaged in a crude method of agriculture. They dwelt in villages with fields adjacent, cultivating maize, beans, and melons as their principal crops. Their methods of culture were primitive, and they rarely produced more than sufficed for their own needs.[19]

The more the natives resorted to agriculture, the less ground they needed for the purpose of hunting. This consideration may partly account for the interest which the Government of the United States took in the civilization of the red man, but such interest was good policy on general principles, for a civilized Indian afforded a less pressing problem than did one in his native simplicity.

During Washington's administration the system of appointing an agent to each of the different tribes was adopted. The agent acted as intermediary between the government and the Indians, attempted to protect them from corruption by supervising their relations with the whites, and tried to promote their civilization by instructing them in agriculture and craftsmanship. The Indians were not allowed to buy whisky from the whites, and the whites were not allowed to live among the Indians except by permission from the agents. Such permits were granted to blacksmiths, carpenters, wheelwrights, and other craftsmen who were needed, but natives were taught the crafts and sometimes were able to supply a large part of the demand for skilled workmen.[20]

The Indians were encouraged by the agents to keep domestic animals and a few of them came to own large herds. They were also instructed in the use of the plow and furnished with seed for planting. The culture of cotton was introduced among them, and they were taught how to use the spinning wheel and the loom. Indeed, some of the native craftsmen learned to make wheels and looms and turned them out in large numbers.

Of all the Indians, the Cherokees most readily took to the ways of civilization. Realizing the futility of resistance, they wished to adjust themselves to the inevitable and through education and industry to fit themselves for citizenship. They took up agriculture so seriously that some of them quit their villages for the purpose of living upon their farms. They kept large numbers of domestic animals and learned to spin and weave. They built roads and erected saw mills and cotton gins. Sequoya, a native Cherokee, invented an alphabet for the use of his people, and they set about diligently to learn to read and write. They even drew up a constitution and instituted a representative government.[21] A census of 1825 shows them, with a population of 15,000, to have possessed 1,300 slaves, 22,000 cattle, over 700 looms, more than 2,000 spinning wheels, nearly 3,000 plows, 10 saw mills, 31 grist mills, 8 cotton gins, 18 ferries, and 18 schools.[22]

The Chickasaws and Choctaws, though somewhat less advanced than the Cherokees, followed their policy of absorbing what civilization they could, and of remaining friendly with the settlers. The Creeks, on the contrary, were warlike and not inclined to adapt themselves to the new situation. The strength of this bellicose confederacy and the fact that its lands bordered upon Spanish Florida may help to explain its relatively independent attitude.

Just before the War of 1812 broke out and Tecumseh undertook to unite all the western Indians against the United States, he visited the Creeks at one of their great councils, and the younger warriors were incited to hostility against the white settlers. Though the older chiefs remained peaceful, the war or "red stick" party was powerful and presently took matters into its own hands.[23]

Florida was still legally in the possession of Spain, but the Napoleonic wars had so shaken the position of that ancient kingdom that her government had fallen prey to French and British armies. The future possession and control of the province became doubtful. President James Madison, fearful for the southern frontier, issued a proclamation in 1810 calling for the occupation of West Florida. At that time, however, it was taken over only as far as the Pearl River. Three years later Mobile was occupied, but Pensacola remained in Spanish hands. To Pensacola a band of the hostile Creeks repaired in 1813 for the purpose of securing munitions of war. The settlers upon the Tombigbee, learning of the expedition, mustered their military strength and marched to meet the Indians as they returned. In the battle of Burnt Corn which followed, the whites drove the Indians from the field, but while the victors were collecting the booty, the Indians rallied, set upon them, and routed their little band.[24]

The isolated Tombigbee settlers recognized this skirmish as the prelude to a bloody Indian war. Seeing no immediate prospect of military assistance, they hurriedly gathered at convenient houses, surrounded them with stockades, and anxiously awaited the movements of the savage warriors. Several hundred men and women were gathered at the home of a wealthy "Indian country-man" named Mims. A stockade was constructed and the place came to be known as Fort Mims, but of military discipline there was little or none. Warned of the presence of Indians, they took no heed and when the savages attacked were utterly unprepared. The defense was desperate but hopeless, and when the day was over there remained only the smoldering ruins and the bodies of the dead. Of all that had been gathered in the fort, only a few escaped.

Appeals for aid were quickly sent to Georgia, Louisiana, and Tennessee, and Andrew Jackson, major-general of the Tennessee militia, collected a force for an expedition. Marching through Huntsville and crossing the Tennessee River where he established Fort Deposit, he entered the country of the Creeks and built Fort Strother upon the upper waters of the Coosa. Often forced to the last extremity by the difficulty of getting supplies and by the restiveness of militia enlisted for short terms of service, Jackson nevertheless cut a road through the wilderness, fought several minor engagements with the savages, and finally reached their principal stronghold at Horseshoe Bend in the Tallapoosa River. Here the Indians had erected a breastwork across the neck of the peninsula formed by the bend of the river. Jackson attacked this work in front while his lieutenant, General John Coffee, approached the bend from the other side of the stream. On this side the Indians had collected a large number of canoes in which to make their escape if it should become necessary; but taking these, Coffee recrossèd the river and attacked the defenders from the rear. Thus trapped, the stubborn resistance of the natives was ineffectual. Some escaped across the river, others were drowned while attempting to get away, and several hundred were left dead upon the field.[25]

The battle of Horseshoe Bend broke the power of the hostile Creeks. Many were dead, and others fled across the Spanish line into Florida. In 1814 the chiefs who remained met Jackson at the confluence of the Coosa and Tallapoosa, where Fort Jackson was erected, and were forced to surrender a broad strip of their land running along the Florida border and all that which lay west of the Coosa River. Thus almost all of the Alabama-Tombigbee basin was cleared of the Indian title and secured for settlement. The Mississippi Territory was indebted to Jackson not only for safety but also for room in which to grow.

That the Southwest was to become a cotton kingdom was foreshadowed by the early history of Madison County. When the old tobacco-growing districts of the southern seaboard began to overflow into the piedmont region, a number of Virginia immigrants established the town of Petersburg where the Broad River flows into the Savannah in Elbert County, Georgia. Here tobacco warehouses were erected and a brisk business ensued. But it did not last long. When the invention of the cotton gin made short staple cotton available for commercial purposes, this crop supplanted tobacco as the principal product of the piedmont region in Georgia and South Carolina. Tobacco warehouses were no longer necessary and Petersburg was abandoned.[26] Its inhabitants were the chief founders of the town of Huntsville.[27] In the small triangle which was the Madison County of that day, nearly 150,000 acres of land were sold between 1809 and 1812.

During this period the sales of land in the Tombigbee settlement were relatively small except that, in 1812 alone, 64,000 acres were disposed of at St. Stephens.

The war naturally halted the progress of the westward movement, but with the coming of peace, the migration was resumed with greatly renewed vigor. The Indians were no longer to be feared, a vast expanse of new territory had been cleared of the native title, cotton was in great demand, and a spirit of adventure and speculation took hold upon the country. In 1816 more than 170,000 acres were sold at St. Stephens.[28]

The territory secured from the Creeks had to be surveyed before it could be placed upon the market, and surveys took time. But the westward rush of land-hungry men did not wait upon the government. Settlers pushed into the country in great numbers. They were usually poor men who had sold all they possessed to secure the necessary means of transportation, and at the end of the journey they sometimes found themselves stranded without food to last until the first crop could be made.[29] There were also land speculators who were engaged in seeking out choice tracts for purchase when the government sales should begin; there were merchants who had brought wagon-loads of goods, which they displayed to the settlers in hastily-erected huts; and there were fugitives from justice seeking refuge in a country where the hand of the law was weak.

Crimes were committed, of course, in such a community as this;[30] and to make the situation worse, those Creeks who had remained friendly to the United States during the war felt, with reason, that they had been unjustly treated when their lands were taken away, and they threatened to give trouble.[31] Since no civil jurisdiction was established in the region, Governor David Holmes of the Mississippi Territory issued a proclamation on June 29, 1815, incorporating the whole of the Creek cession as Monroe County.[32]

This action was not in accord with the ideas of the government, for an act of 1807 had forbidden intrusion upon the public lands. In accordance with this act, President Madison issued a proclamation in December, 1815, ordering the removal of squatters and authorizing the use of military force to accomplish that purpose.[33] Some ejections were made, but Congress heard the plea of the squatters and, by an act of April 26, 1816, those who had come in before February of that year were to be allowed to remain until the land upon which they were settled should be sold.[34]

On the north and west, the Creek cession overlapped lands claimed by the Choctaw, Chickasaw, and Cherokee Indians. The government commissioned Andrew Jackson to treat with these tribes for their claims to the disputed areas, and treaties providing for the relinquishment of all three tracts were drawn up in

FIGURE 1: Indian cessions in the Mississippi Territory

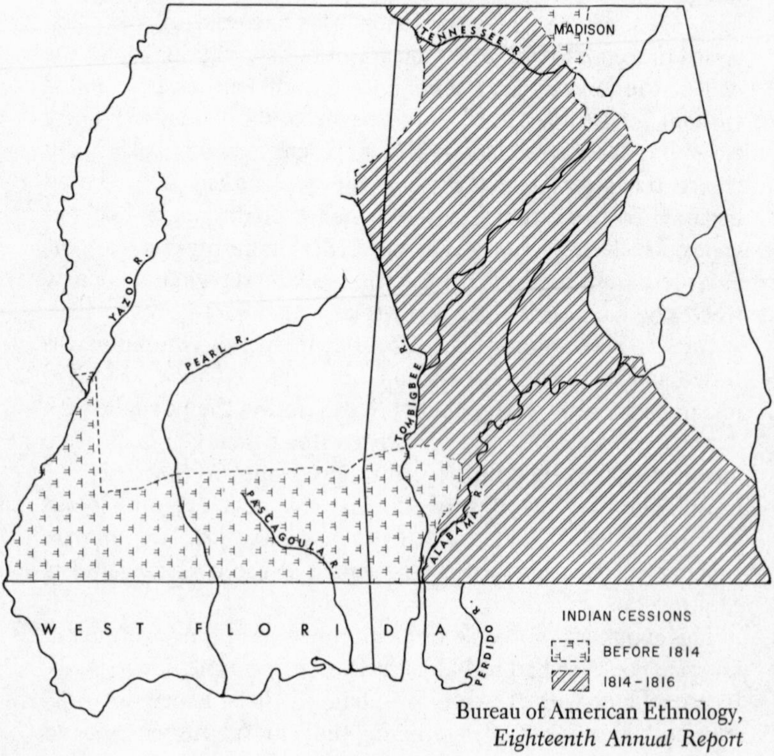

Bureau of American Ethnology,
Eighteenth Annual Report

1816. This cleared up the Indian title to the greater part of that territory which was soon to become the State of Alabama. The Creeks still held the entire tract lying east of the Coosa River; the Cherokees held the northeastern corner above this, the Chickasaws held a small tract in the northwestern corner; and the Choctaws retained a small acreage west of the Tombigbee.[35] (See figure 1.)

On May 9, 1817, Governor Holmes issued a proclamation creating three new counties which included the new cessions and a part of the Creek cession. Elk County was to comprise the land lying north of the Tennessee River and west of Madison County; Blount County was to be made up of that lying south of the Tennessee and north of the watershed between that river and the Alabama-Tombigbee basin; and Shelby County was to comprise the area lying south of Blount County bounded on the west by the Tombigbee, on the south by Clarke County, and on the east by the watershed between the Tombigbee and Alabama rivers.[36] But the act dividing the Territory had already been passed by Congress, and these three counties never had a concrete existence. An Elk County is sometimes enumerated in the early gazetteers, and a Blount and a Shelby County were established in the Alabama Territory in 1818, but they have no continuity with those established by Governor Holmes.

CHAPTER TWO

The New Country

THE NEW COUNTRY[1] WHICH WAS SOON TO BE-
come Alabama is divided, from an agricultural point of view, into
three principal regions: the Tennessee Valley, the Alabama-
Tombigbee basin, and the central hilly region which separates
the two. Fed by streams which drain the country as far north as
the Tennessee Valley, the Alabama and Tombigbee rivers tra-
verse the central and southwestern portions of the area, and
empty their united waters into Mobile Bay. In the early days of
Alabama, these streams furnished the only good commercial highway into the state. They bound her southern section into one
cotton-growing community, and their fertile bottom lands furnished the most desirable fields for the planter of the staple.

The central hilly region is drained by southward-flowing
streams which are not navigable, and the inaccessibility of the
region, together with the rugged nature of the land, prevented it
from attaining agricultural importance. Yet the isolated valleys
were often fertile, and a scattered population maintained frontier
conditions here for a long time.

Making a large bend across the northern end of Alabama, the
Tennessee River flows through a wide and fertile valley. During
the early days the produce of this region had to be floated down
the long and tortuous courses of the Tennessee and Mississippi
rivers to New Orleans, but the soil was fertile and from the very
first, attracted planters in large numbers.

Looked at in more detail, the surface of Alabama is divided into several areas differing in formation and fertility of soil.[2] (See figure 2.) Entering the northeastern corner of the state with the Tennessee River and running down toward the center is the

FIGURE 2: Geological map of Alabama

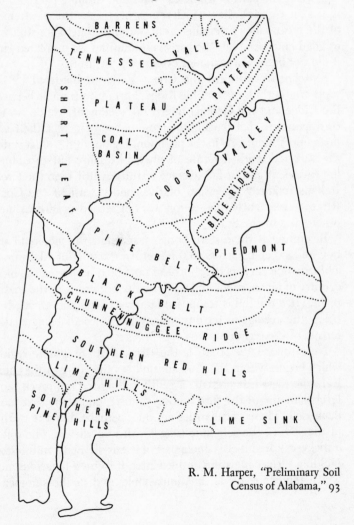

R. M. Harper, "Preliminary Soil
Census of Alabama," 93

southern extremity of the Cumberland Plateau. Here the ridges run in long sweeps and give a really mountainous aspect to the region. Lookout Mountain is the most pronounced of the highlands. South of the Tennessee Valley the ridges give way to the broken hills of the north-central portion of the state.

Skirting the plateau to the eastward and running parallel with it, lies the Coosa Valley, which represents the southern extremity of the great valley extending from Virginia. There are stretches of good land here, but the early communities were isolated, and it did not become a region of extensive agriculture.

Still farther eastward the Coosa Valley is bordered by the southern foothills of the Blue Ridge. Forming a triangle between the Ridge and the Georgia line is the piedmont section, which corresponds to that skirting the mountains in Georgia, the Carolinas, and Virginia. As in the piedmont regions of the older states, the stiff, red lands here are of unequal quality but capable of improvement and of fair average fertility. Until 1836 the Creek Indians retained possession of the country east of the Coosa River; consequently this section was not settled as early as most other parts of the State.

Beginning at the eastern border just below the piedmont section and sweeping across to the northwest corner of Alabama in a broadening curve is the short-leaf pine belt, bordering the older country of igneous rock and marking the beginning of the coastal plain. Here the soil is composed largely of sand and gravel. It is below the average in fertility, rolling piney woods being characteristic of the region.

Next toward the south is the Black Belt[3] or prairie region, which begins within the state and follows the curve of the short-leaf pine region. It presents a gently rolling terrain, much more level than any of the surrounding country, and somewhat more depressed. These peculiarities are due, perhaps, like the quality of the soil, to the soft limestone which underlies it. The soil is a sticky, calcareous clay, and a part of it was originally unforested. Holding surface moisture in the winter, it forms a tenacious mud which renders roads all but impassable, and in the summer it bakes to a hard crust. A description of this region given by one of the early settlers in 1821 affords a graphic idea of the appearance of the country:

Wherever these prairies exist, the lime is this soft consistence, when it approaches near the surface, the soil appears whitish, and is clothed with a short growth of grass and herbage; where it lies deeper the grass is denser and taller, and upon the borders, between the wood land and prairies, the growth of weeds and grass is very luxuriant. But upon the prairies themselves, there is not sufficient depth of earth for the growth of trees. Such is the checkered and diversified appearance of this part of the country where those prairies exist. Fancy yourself for a moment in such a situation; before you a wide and extended meadow, to the right and left intervening strips of oaks and pines; proceeding onwards, the prospect seems terminated by the surrounding woods; anon, you catch a glimpse of the opening vista; and now again the prospect expands into the wide spread horizon of an extensive prairie. These prairies are generally rolling; which is a great advantage, as otherwise they retain water, to the great injury of the crops; and as it respects the quality of the soil, it is generally admitted that it is the best the country affords. . . . The only objection to these prairies is, the scarcity of good water. . . .[4]

The relative scarcity of running water, together with other disadvantages, were special problems to the farmer, and the towns which grew up in connection with the cotton industry here—Montgomery, Selma, and others—are located on the edge of the prairie rather than within it. Though the planters at first sought the river bottoms and avoided the prairie, the latter came after 1830 to be looked upon as the best cotton land in the state. As late as 1880 it formed the principal cotton producing area of Alabama.

Montgomery County has always been a cotton-planting center, and its early history is illustrative of such settlements. Almost the entire area of the country consists of fine prairie lands which extend in long, unbroken stretches of fertile fields. But the Alabama River, which forms its northern boundary, is bordered by bottom land which is not of the prairie type. A map of the county, made up from the land records and showing the dates at which the tracts were purchased from the government, brings out the fact that the great majority of the settlements before 1821 was located in the river bottom area. By 1828 encroachments were being made upon the prairie, but the greater part of it was still unsettled. On the other hand, in Clarke County, at the confluence of the Alabama and Tombigbee rivers, there were extensive settlements before 1821, though very few between that year and 1828. In Dallas and Perry counties where there is both river and prairie land, the river bottoms and the red lands bordering the prairies were taken up, but few settlements were made in the prairies before the end of 1828.[5]

The Black Belt is bordered on the south by the Chunnennuggee Ridge. This runs across the state in a narrow strip, but toward the eastern border where the Black Belt dwindles away, the ridge broadens and replaces it. A limestone formation underlies this section, but it is different from that of the prairie region in being of normal hardness. This accounts for the fact that the ridge country rises distinctly above the prairie, and that its surface is of a relatively rugged character. The soil is predominantly a sandy loam and is, like that of the Black Belt, above the average in fertility. It was also a good cotton growing region.

Below the Chunnennuggee Ridge and extending to the southern border of the state, lie the southern red hill[6] and southern pine hill regions. Between these lie two small calcareous areas, but there are no marked transitions in the surface here. The appearance of the country and the nature of the soil are so fairly uniform that from an agricultural standpoint these areas might be considered together.

In the region of the red hills the surface is broken and rises almost to mountainous ruggedness in places. One of the two railroad tunnels in the whole coastal plain lies in this section. Pine predominates over other forest trees, and the soil is reddish sandy clay. Its fertility is only average, but fertilizers can be used to advantage.

Proceeding toward the coast, the hills become less pronounced and the long-leaf pine predominates. The character of the soil does not change materially; it is relatively infertile, but subject to improvement by artificial fertilization.

It is worthy of note that in the Gulf coastal plain there is nothing corresponding to the pine barrens of the South Atlantic states. The reddish sandy clay prevails all the way to the coast, and the surface presents a rolling and often a rugged appearance.

CHAPTER THREE

The Immigrants

During the latter half of the seventeenth century, England was developing the spinning and weaving machinery which played such a large part in bringing about the Industrial Revolution. The increased demand for raw cotton which resulted from this development was answered in 1793 by Eli Whitney's invention of the cotton gin. Until this time, it was necessary to separate the lint from the seed by hand or by means of a pair of simple rollers. The black-seeded sea-island, or long staple, cotton was the only variety amenable to such processes, for its long fibre did not cling closely to the seed and could be removed easily. The short staple of the green-seeded variety clung so closely to the seed that it could not be removed profitably by the simple processes in use.

Long staple cotton could be raised only along the coast and on the bordering sea-islands of Georgia and South Carolina. The short staple cotton, on the other hand, could be raised in the uplands, and when the invention of the cotton gin rendered the culture of this variety profitable, the Georgia and South Carolina piedmont supplanted the tidewater as the principal cotton-producing area.[1]

This region has been settled largely by men from Virginia and Pennsylvania. The culture of tobacco was the main industry for some years, but when upland cotton was introduced it quickly came to predominate. Towns founded for the warehousing and inspection of tobacco, like Petersburg, were abandoned because their facilities were no longer necessary.[2] Many inhabitants moved to Madison County.

That the spread of cotton culture into the Southwest was inevitable is indicated by its early introduction into the Mississippi Territory. This natural movement was interrupted by the War of 1812, but its pent-up force was precipitated by conditions following the end of the struggle. In England, where the source of supply was cut off during the War, the price of the staple rose to an abnormal level, while in America the price fell off sharply because the usual market was gone. When peace was made and normal trade relations were resumed with the lifting of the blockade of our coast, England again obtained her supply of American cotton and the price in this country rose immediately, the average for 1815 being almost thirty cents a pound.[3]

To the favorable price was added the inducement of new lands cleared of the Indian title during the War and the innate restlessness of the population. Sales of newly surveyed land were opened at St. Stephens during the latter part of 1815, and the following year over 100,000 acres were disposed of by the government.[4] No sales were made in the new Creek cession until 1817, but in that year $750,000 worth of these lands were sold.[5]

The old Georgia-South Carolina piedmont region had two distinct disadvantages from the cotton planter's point of view. Its soil was not considered as fertile as that of the Alabama river bottoms and prairies; and it lacked transportation facilities, being cut off from the tidewater by the broad pine barrens and being without navigable rivers. Thus, before the culture of upland cotton had reached anything like a mature development in these regions, it began to be transferred to the new Southwest. Population flowed from the older states into the pioneer country until the drain was keenly felt in the deserted communities.

Though the statement cannot be backed by statistics, it appears that the majority of the planters who moved westward with their slaves came from the piedmont rather than from the tidewater regions of the South Atlantic states.[6] The tidewater had its staple crops of tobacco, rice, and sea-island cotton, which were not disturbed by the new developments. The planters here were usually well established, their investment was heavy, and their land had a certain monopoly value. Their slaves could still be employed more or less profitably, and their social position tended to hold them where they were. Thus few people of extensive wealth moved into the Alabama region during the period of early settlement. Only the man who needed to better his fortune had an inducement to make the necessary sacrifice. Any who owned slaves usually had only a small number, and many who later became planters had no slaves at all to begin with. In other words, the small farmer of the piedmont region became the pioneer planter of the Southwest.

When a man prepared to transplant his establishment, he usually sold the land he held and retained the proceeds for the purchase of his new domain. His household goods and farm implements were packed on wagons and started the trek over the rough road toward the new home. The slaves drove the herds of cattle and hogs, while the planter's family brought up the rear in a carriage.[7] It was a tedious journey, the roads being merely clearings though the forest without bridges. The smaller streams were forded, and crude ferries were established at the larger ones. Yet there were compensations; hunting along the way afforded diversions for the men, and the campfire about which the wayfarers gathered at night shed a romantic glow upon the faces of those who were traveling into a strange land.

Having reached the place where he was to make his home, the planter constructed a log cabin after the usual manner. Two rooms were built opposite each other and joined by a passage-way. Chimneys built of stones or clay-daubed sticks were put up at opposite ends of the structure and great open fireplaces served for both heating and cooking. A lean-to might be attached behind one or both of the rooms, and there was an attic above. Before the introduction of saw mills, the floors were made of puncheons —logs split in halves with the flat side upward. The chinks between the logs were filled with clay, the doors and shutters were of crude boards, and the shingles were hand-split. In such a dwelling, the planter who brought his household furnishings could establish a kind of rude comfort which sufficed even the wealthiest immigrants during the first few years of their sojourn. The first and only governor of the Alabama Territory lived in such a log cabin during the years of his administration and until his premature death.[8]

But not all the newcomers were even thus fortunately situated. No very extensive tracts of the new land were offered for sale before 1818, and men who had homes to sell in the old states would naturally wish to purchase a location in the new country before moving. Yet, from 1815 onward, men poured into the ceded lands and "squatted" upon them in spite of the law and the government.[9] It was the policy of the United States to prevent intrusion until surveys could be made and the lands offered for sale at auction. Attempts were made to remove the squatters; troops were called in and ordered to burn the cabins of those who refused to leave, but it was all of no avail.[10]

Men of this class, being improvident by nature, did not come to seek wealth but merely to gain a subsistence or to enjoy the freedom of the forest. They built their simple cabins and planted their crops of corn between trees which they killed by girdling. Their greatest immediate problem was to live until the first crop was made, and here there was much difficulty.[11]

The influx of immigrants was so great in 1816 and 1817 that the Indians and scattered pioneers were not able to furnish enough corn to meet the needs of the newcomers. In 1816 corn brought $4.00 a bushel along the road from Huntsville to Tuscaloosa,[12] and so scarce did the grain become among the local Indians that the government had to come to their rescue in 1817 in order to relieve actual distress.[13]

Where did the various immigrants who entered the Alabama country come from? By what routes did they reach their destination; and in what part of the Territory did they settle? Although statistics cannot be produced, a fairly reliable idea may be gained from various accounts which, in the main, agree.

The two roads through the Mississippi Territory for which Congress made appropriations in 1806 were continuations of established routes of travel.[14] (See figure 3.) That from Nashville to Natchez, the Natchez Trace, was a continuation of the Kentucky Trace which passed from Nashville through Lexington, to Maysville, and thence by the Old National Road through Columbus, Zanesville, and Wheeling to Pittsburgh. The Natchez Trace was the principal highway for the region it traversed, but it was hardly more than a bridle path through the woods.

The route from Athens to New Orleans, the Federal Road, followed the direction of the Alabama River and passed through the Tombigbee settlements.[15] Beyond Athens, the route passed northeastward through Greenville, Salisbury, Charlotte, and Fredericksburg, to Washington, Baltimore, and Philadelphia.

FIGURE 3: Road map, 1818

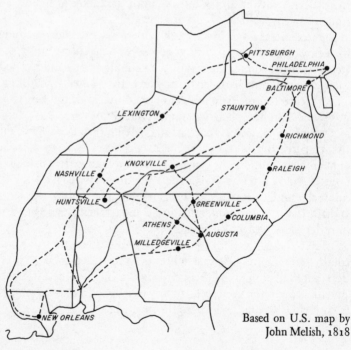

Based on U.S. map by
John Melish, 1818

Thus it traversed the piedmont region of the South Atlantic states and connected the Southwest with the commercial centers of the East. Diverging from this route just beyond the Georgia line, another highway passed eastward of it and connected the southern capitals which stood at the fall line of the rivers flowing into the Atlantic. Extending through Milledgeville, Augusta, Columbia, Raleigh, and Richmond, this again united with the piedmont route just before reaching Washington.

But there was still another means of access to the Alabama country which was of great importance. A road which branched off from the Pittsburgh-Philadelphia highway passed southwestward through the Valley of Virginia and then followed the course of the Holston River to Knoxville. From Knoxville the original highway passed westward to Nashville, but with the formation of Madison County, a spur was extended southward to Huntsville, and this soon came to be an important route of travel.

Now a man coming into Alabama from the piedmont region of Georgia would have the choice of two routes. He could go by the Federal Road into the Alabama-Tombigbee basin, or he could take a road which passed from Augusta to Athens, crossed the Tennessee River where Chattanooga now stands, and led on to Nashville.[16] The highway crossed the road from Knoxville to Huntsville and gave access to the fertile Tennessee Valley region. The Georgia men who helped to settle Madison County in 1809 took this route,[17] but the later emigration of Georgia planters was mostly into the southern part of Alabama, and they passed along the Federal Road.

The first lands of the Creek cession which were put on sale were disposed of at Milledgeville, Georgia, and they lay along the upper course of the Alabama River in the neighborhood of what was to be Montgomery County.[18] It is easy to understand, therefore, how it was that the Georgia planters established a predominance in this region from the first. With this group as a nucleus, the immigrants from Georgia, apparently following the route of the Federal Road, came to form perhaps the strongest element in the population of all the southeastern counties of Alabama.[19] (See figure 4.)

FIGURE 4: Origin of population

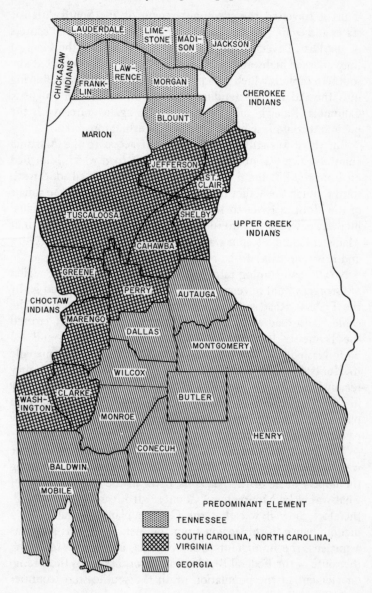

PREDOMINANT ELEMENT

TENNESSEE

SOUTH CAROLINA, NORTH CAROLINA, VIRGINIA

GEORGIA

Men from the piedmont region of South Carolina had two routes open to them. They could take the fall-line road through Columbia or the piedmont road through Greenville and reach the Alabama basin by the Federal Road. But if they wished to reach the Tennessee Valley, they could pass northward from Greenville, through Saluda Gap in the Blue Ridge where it borders North and South Carolina, then to the site of Asheville, and along the course of the French Broad to Knoxville, and thence to Huntsville.[20] Immigrants came by both of these routes, and, appearing to have avoided the settlements of those who had preceded them in the Tennessee Valley and in the Alabama River basin, the majority passed on from both directions into the central hilly region or the basin of the Black Warrior and upper Tombigbee rivers.

Migrants from North Carolina could have taken the route along the French Broad to Knoxville and thence to Huntsville, but since this road traversed only the mountainous western region of the state, it is probable that most of them thought the highway from Raleigh through Columbus and Augusta to the Federal Road more convenient. These men, like those from South Carolina, found the central region of Alabama most attractive.

The Virginians who came from the Valley followed their highway through Cumberland Gap and down the Holston to Knoxville, thence gaining access to the Tennessee Valley. Some of these passed on down to the Black Warrior and Tombigbee valleys. For Virginians from the piedmont region, it was more convenient to take one of the eastern roads leading to southern Alabama, whence they could make their way into the Tombigbee-Warrior region if they so desired.

Of course the Tennessee Valley was most easily accessible to the men just over the line, and consequently Tennesseeans had a predominance in this section. Some bought lands in the Valley, while others passed beyond into the hilly region and became squatters upon the National Domain, for the greater part of the lands in the Valley were put upon the market in 1818 but those south of it were not sold for some years afterward. Here backwoods communities were established in the isolated valleys, and frontier conditions of life prevailed for a long time.

The principal route of travel connecting the Tennessee Valley with the Alabama-Tombigbee region was a road passing southwestward from Huntsville through Jones Valley to the town of Tuscaloosa, which grew up at the head of boat navigation upon the Black Warrior. It was along this route that the principal settlements were made in the central hilly region. At first the Tennesseeans predominated here, but South Carolinians soon came in such numbers as to exceed the Tennesseeans in some localities. The struggle for supremacy between these elements in Blount and Jefferson counties provoked open hostilities before it was settled. In the end, the Tennesseans came to predominate in Blount, while the South Carolinians had the majority in Jefferson County.[21]

Most communities had their local color, and the state one came from was always a matter of significance. In the Tombigbee-Warrior region, North Carolinians, South Carolinians, and Virginians mingled in varying proportions, but together formed a predominating population element which had its own characteristics. As late as 1856, Greene County, at the conjunction of the Black Warrior with the Tombigbee, had a population of 438 native South Carolinians, 357 Alabamians, 348 North Carolinians, 92 Georgians, 45 Tennesseeans, 24 Kentuckians, 12 men from Connecticut, 37 from Ireland, and 10 from Germany.[22]

The presence of a small number of foreigners is characteristic of the early period, and so is the presence of New Englanders. The cosmopolitan population was confined to the trading towns where the merchants were largely Yankees.[23] This was especially true of Mobile, founded by the French in 1702 and plagued with a transient population that was turbulent and varied. In 1714 Jean Baptiste de Bienville, the leader of this settlement, had founded Fort Toulouse near the present site of Wetumpka and in 1736 Fort Tombecbé near the confluence of the Warrior and Tombigbee rivers. These strongholds were for protection against the red man and to further Indian trade as well as for a buffer against the English. However, the Mobile settlers hugged the coast for decade after decade and never penetrated the vast northward sweep of the forest. A community of Germans was established at Dutch Bend on the Alabama River;[24] and Demopolis, on the Tombigbee, was founded by a band of Napoleonic refugees, but such segregated community-building was not characteristic.

Finally, in spite of the mixture which was produced by the flow of immigration into Alabama, three areas were distinguished for peculiarities caused partly by the predominant element in the population. In the Tennessee Valley the preponderance of Tennesseeans gave a strongly democratic flavor to political ideas; in the Tombigbee-Warrior region, the Carolina-Virginia predominance seems to have encouraged a flavor of conservatism in things political; while the influence of Georgia politics is clearly discernible in Montgomery County. Nevertheless other factors played a more important part in shaping opinions and politics than did the geographical origin of the people, the effect of which, indeed, was often entirely obliterated.

CHAPTER FOUR

The Division of the Territory

THE QUESTION OF THE DIVISION OF THE TERRI-
tory came up as early as 1803, for in that year the Tombigbee
settlers sent a petition to Congress praying that they might be
separated from the community upon the Mississippi.[1] The petition was renewed in 1809, the petitioners stating that they had
a government in name only and that they were entirely neglected
by the authorities of the Territory.[2] This attitude was perfectly
natural, for the Tombigbee settlement was widely separated from
that around Natchez, and, being in a minority in the legislature,
it was unable to make its needs felt at so great a distance.

In 1809, Madison County was opened up in the Tennessee
Valley, and in 1810 West Florida was annexed to the United
States. This country was claimed as a part of the Louisiana purchase, but the title was most flimsy. Nevertheless, war with England threatened, and since French and English armies were
fighting over the throne of Spain, West Florida in Spanish hands
was a menace to the southern coast. England might use the Gulf
ports as a base through which to treat with hostile Indians, and
thereby the situation of the frontier settlements in this region
would be rendered critical in case of hostilities. A declaration of
independence by a band of men, largely Americans, who had
migrated into West Florida, gave President Madison the excuse
which he eagerly accepted as a way out of the difficult situation.
By proclamation he declared the Spanish province annexed to

the United States, and Governor William C. C. Claiborne of the Territory of Orleans, took formal possession of the country as far east as the Pearl River.[3]

The newly-acquired region was joined to the Territory of Orleans for administrative purposes. In 1811, this Territory became the state of Louisiana, and more than 400 West Floridians petitioned Congress that their district be annexed to the Mississippi Territory.[4] Until this time the Mississippi delegate had been working in Congress for admission to the Union without division, but here the intersectional rivalry in Congress came into play. The House, where the North was in the majority, showed itself even at this early date willing to provide for the admission of the undivided Territory. But in the Senate the South, having lost its hold upon the House, was trying to maintain an equality. This could be accomplished only by the admission of a slave state every time a free state was admitted, and from this point of view, it was desirable to carve as many states as possible from southern territory. Consequently, the Senate insisted that the Mississippi Territory be divided.

The combination of this situation with the West Florida annexation suggested a new idea to George Poindexter, the territorial delegate, and he brought forward a proposition for division by a line running due east from the mouth of the Yazoo. The southern portion, with West Florida annexed, was to be admitted to the Union at once, while the northern portion was to be given a territorial government.[5]

This move called down a storm upon the author's head. The Madison County inhabitants would, it is true, have been glad enough to see the plan carried through, leaving them with a territorial government to administer alone.[6] But to be tied permanently to the Mississippi River region with its separate interests was the last thing desired by the Tombigbee settlers. Opposition was quickly expressed in this quarter, and it was seconded by many in the Natchez region who felt that the frontier settlements were yet too young to support the burden of state government.[7]

There were other reasons, too, why many opposed the institution of state government at this time. In 1795 the legislature of Georgia had made large grants of land in the Mississippi country to certain speculating companies which came to be known as the "Yazoo" land companies. Extensive graft in connection with the deal having been exposed, the next session of the legislature repealed the grants and deprived the companies of their charters. This was supposed to have ended the matter, but in 1809 the Supreme Court of the United States, in the case of *Fletcher* vs. *Peck,* declared that the repeal of the grants was a breach of contract, and therefore forbidden by the Constitution. The claimants under the companies at once appealed to Congress for relief, but John Randolph of Roanoke made the case his pet antipathy and prevented anything being done until 1814.

When, in 1802, Georgia ceded to the United States her claim to the Mississippi region, it was provided in the agreement that all completed British and Spanish grants should be valid. Actual settlers were to be provided for, and all claims arising under the Georgia act which established Bourbon County in the ceded region also were to be validated. In addition to this, 5,000,000 acres of land were set aside for the satisfaction of any other claimants under acts of Georgia, to be appropriated as Congress might see fit. The Yazoo claimants were the chief possible beneficiaries under this provision, but it was long before the matter was put at rest.[8]

In 1811 many titles to land in the Mississippi Territory were threatened by the Yazoo claimants, and many others were threatened by a conflict between British and Spanish grants. A number of actual settlers held tracts under Spanish grants which had been superseded by grants under the British administration. These British claims had never been established, but the matter was subject to judicial determination, and it caused uneasiness to many who lived upon the land.

Because of this uncertainty of land tenure, courts of federal jurisdiction were not established in the Mississippi Territory, and though the delegate in Congress pressed for a compromise of the

British claims, nothing had been accomplished at the time Mississippi was admitted to the Union. It was the dread of federal courts, therefore, and of British and Yazoo claimants which caused many men to oppose admission to statehood in 1812.[9]

But in spite of all these objections, an act providing for the admission of the undivided Territory was passed by the House and sent up to the Senate in this year. The Senate committee to which the bill was referred advised division along the line of the Tombigbee River and proposed that the question lie over until the next session.[10]

Georgia, in ceding her claim to the United States, had provided that the whole Territory be admitted into the Union as a single state as soon as its population should amount to 60,000 whites. In view of the action of the Senate, Poindexter now brought in a resolution that Congress secure Georgia's permission to a division of the Territory.[11] The resolution passed both Houses, and within the year Georgia's acquiescence was reported to the Senate. But the War of 1812 coming on at this time, its ensuing depression was added to the arguments of those who wished to postpone the question of statehood. Thus, from 1812 to 1815 the matter was little agitated.

When the question of admission was again brought before Congress in 1815, two things had happened to change the situation. Though General James Wilkinson did not occupy Mobile until the following year, in 1812 as much of West Florida as lay between the Pearl and Perdido rivers was added to the Territory, and in 1814 Congress settled the Yazoo claims by appropriating $5,000,000 in scrip to be distributed to the claimants under the several companies and redeemed in payment on the first lands to be sold in the Mississippi territory.

Though the British claims still threatened many of the settlers, the prospects of peace and immigration now caused the new territorial delegate, Dr. William D. Lattimore, who had opposed admission when first elected in 1813, to come out in favor of admission without division.[12] Petitions to that effect were sent up by the legislature, and in 1816 the House passed a bill framed in accordance with that policy. But the attitude of the Senate had not changed. The committee to which the bill was referred again proposed division by a north and south line, and the question of admission was once more postponed.[13]

Lattimore now saw the futility of working along the old line and expressed himself willing to accept division if Congress insisted upon it.[14] In the meantime, the situation had changed at home. The extensive Creek cession of 1814 and the smaller cessions from the Cherokees, Chickasaws, and Choctaws in 1816 had opened up a vast stretch of country comprising most of the eastern part of the Territory. The settlers upon the Tombigbee now expected to see their river basin become, in a short while, more populous than the region bordering the Mississippi. They accordingly anticipated control of the legislature and the removal of the capital to St. Stephens.

Such a prospect was by no means pleasing to the men who lived between the Pearl River and the Mississippi. So greatly did they dread the threatened preponderance of the eastern section of the Territory that they gave up their old enthusiasm for a single state and supported Lattimore on the question of division. This, they now believed, was the only way to keep their capital near the banks of the Mississippi.

On the other hand, the Tombigbee settlers now appeared much alarmed at the prospect of division. Meetings were held in several places, and the counties were urged to send delegates to assemble in convention at Ford's on Pearl River. Here a gathering of delegates took place in October, but Madison and the counties west of the Pearl were not represented. Resolutions opposing division were drawn up and Judge Harry Toulmin was sent to Washington to present the memorial of the convention and to support it when the matter should be brought up again.[15]

When Congress assembled in December, the House committee to which the Mississippi question was referred expressed itself as being in favor of a division of the Territory, with immediate admission of the western portion and a territorial government for the eastern half. The demarcation line now became the disputed point. Lattimore proposed a line running due north from the Gulf to the northwest corner of Washington County, then following the Choctaw boundary to the Tombigbee. Toulmin wished a line that would give Wayne, Greene, and Jackson counties to the eastern government, and some attempt was made to fix upon the Pascagoula as the boundary. The counties in question were much nearer the Tombigbee than they were to the Mississippi, and it was argued that it would be an unnecessary inconvenience to their inhabitants to have to look to a capital upon the Great River when St. Stephens was so much closer.[16] In the end, Lattimore was more successful than Toulmin and, though giving some ground, he came close to having his way. The line was fixed so as to run due north from the Gulf to the northwest corner of Washington County, thence directly to the point where Bear Creek flows into the Tennessee, and then along the course of the river to the Tennessee line.

It will be noticed that the present boundary does not run due north from the Gulf, but slightly northwest instead. This is because it was found that the line, as originally established, encroached slightly upon Wayne, Greene, and Jackson counties. In order to remedy the encroachment, the Alabama enabling act of 1819 changed the line so as to make it run southeastward from the northwest corner of Washington County and to strike the Gulf at a point ten miles east of the mouth of the Pascagoula.[17]

The act establishing the Alabama Territory was approved March 3, 1817.[18] All laws applying to the old Mississippi Territory were to remain in force for the present. Officials under the old government for eastern districts were to retain their positions until they should be replaced, and William Wyatt Bibb of Georgia was appointed governor.

Bibb had just previously resigned his seat in the United States Senate because his vote for a bill increasing the salaries of senators aroused a storm of indignation at home. His colleague, Charles Tait, was under the same condemnation, but, urged by John W. Walker of Huntsville, he remained until the end of his term and saw Alabama safely admitted to the Union. Then, retiring from public life in Georgia, he purchased a plantation upon the Alabama and moved into the new state.[19] It was Senator

Tait, who, in 1802, had notified the Senate of Georgia's consent to a division of the Mississippi Territory and who piloted through that body the final bill which provided for division in 1817. Both Tait and Bibb were staunch friends of William H. Crawford of Georgia, Secretary of the Treasury, and it was probably through his influence that the latter was appointed governor of the Alabama Territory.

Such members as had represented eastern districts in the legislature of the Mississippi Territory were empowered to meet at St. Stephens to set the new government in motion. There, on January 19, 1818, the first session was held. St. Stephens stood at the head of schooner navigation on the Tombigbee. In 1811 it consisted of three houses; four years later it boasted of nine; and in 1816 the number had grown to forty.[20] In two rooms hired for the purpose in the Douglas Hotel, the legislature met.[21] The House had about thirteen members who elected Gabriel Moore its speaker. The Council had but one member, James Titus, who had been president of the old Council. Not to be abashed by the situation, he convened with all due ceremony, dispatched business, and adjourned from day to day.[22]

In his message the governor recommended the promotion of education and internal improvements, but added that the latter object could hardly be accomplished without the aid of the federal government. Accordingly, a memorial asking for assistance in this matter was drawn up by the legislature and sent to Washington. The legislation accomplished at this session included the establishment of new counties; the incorporation of a steamboat company, an academy, and a bank at St. Stephens; and the repeal of the law fixing a maximum rate of interest which could be charged on loans. Thereafter, any percentage agreed upon between the contracting parties and stated in writing would be legal. Six men were nominated from whom the Council president was to select three for the Executive Council, and a commission was appointed to report to the next session of the legislature on a favorable site for the permanent seat of the territorial government.[23]

It was during the territorial period of Alabama that the Seminole War broke out on the Florida frontier. Several white settlers were killed by the restive Indians, and militia was rushed to the seat of disturbance. Though troops were stationed at a number of points in Alabama, and a certain amount of fighting took place within her borders, the struggle went on primarily in Florida. The storm stirred up by Jackson's unauthorized attack upon Pensacola and by the hanging of Alexander Arbuthnot and Robert Ambrister, British subjects found guilty of inciting the Indians to revolt, belong to national rather than to state history.

Alabama was not greatly affected by these events and the tide of immigration moved on undisturbed. Among those who came in about this time was a party of Frenchmen, supporters of Napoleon, fleeing from the Bourbons who had been returned to power. They had moved to America in a body and formed an association with headquarters at Philadelphia. Inquiring for land where the vine and the olive might be grown, their attention had been directed to Alabama. At their request, Congress agreed to sell two townships of land at the confluence of the Black Warrior and the Tombigbee. Here a town was laid out and a settlement established, but these aristocratic, homesick exiles had little heart and less pocket for cultivating the vine and the olive in such uncongenial surroundings. With the Tri-color proudly flying over a log cabin, the refugees, clad in the elegant uniforms of French army officers, went about their humble tasks of carving homes out of the Alabama forest. Their leader was General Charles Lefebvre Desnouettes, who had been with Napoleon on his disastrous march against Moscow. In the colony were other high ranking officers who had shared Napoleon's bloody campaigns, among them General Count Bertrand Clausel and Colonel Nicholas Raoul. The latter had accompanied Napoleon to Elba. The exiles found it impossible to graft their ancient culture onto the primitive, inhospitable wilderness, and the undertaking failed. Their venture is enshrined in the name they gave the county in which their settlement was located—Marengo.[24]

CHAPTER FIVE

Alabama Becomes a State

So RAPID HAD BEEN THE GROWTH OF POPULATION in Alabama during 1817 and 1818 that, when the second session of the legislature met at St. Stephens in November of the latter year, transition to statehood was expected within a short while. Preparations for this event consequently absorbed the attention of the assembly.

A petition to Congress praying that the Territory be admitted to the Union as a state was drawn up by the legislature and sent by John W. Walker, the new speaker of the House, to his friend, Senator Tait of Georgia,[1] who presented it to the Senate. But the matter was not allowed to rest here. A census of the Territory had been taken, and the legislature proceeded to apportion the representatives for the constitutional convention. On this question considerable difficulty arose. Madison was the most populous county in the Territory and the members from the southern counties attempted to reduce the representation of the Tennessee Valley region by providing that no county could have more than a given number of seats in the convention. This was strongly opposed by members from the northern counties, who finally carried their point and secured a proportional representation. But in order to accomplish this it became necessary for them to accept a rider to the apportionment bill providing for the location of the seat of government in the southern part of the Territory.[2]

The first session of the territorial legislature had appointed a committee which was to report on a suitable site for the seat of government. At the second session, Governor Bibb, who was on the committee and seems to have taken the entire responsibility of the choice upon himself, reported in favor of locating the capital at the junction of the Cahawba and Alabama rivers.[3] The place selected, while in agreement with the compromise and convenient for all those who lived on the rivers of southern Alabama, was quite out of communication with the Tennessee Valley, and naturally was opposed by the men from that section. In giving their consent to the bill which established this location as the capital, the representatives from the northern counties made a susbstantial concession, but by way of compensation, they secured a provision stipulating that Huntsville would be the temporary seat of government until a town could be laid out and buildings erected at Cahawba.

Walker kept Tait posted on all these proceedings. He sent him a copy of the apportionment bill, stating that the Senate was expected to distribute the seats in the constitutional convention accordingly, and that Huntsville would be the place of meeting.[4] John Crowell had been sent to Washington as territorial delegate, but his influence is to be seen in none of these transactions. Indeed, Walker wrote to Tait that he did not hold a very high opinion of the delegate,[5] and there is evidence to show that Crowell, in so far as he was able to bring any weight to bear, opposed the plans of Walker and Tait.[6] However, the Senator from Georgia succeeded in getting his enabling act through as desired, and it was signed on March 2, 1819.[7] The convention was to meet in Huntsville on the first Monday in July, with Madison County securing eight delegates against four for the next largest county. Provision was made for granting to the new state the sixteenth section of land in each township for the use of schools; all salt springs within her borders; 3.0 percent of the proceeds of all sales of public lands within the state to be applied in the construction of roads; two townships for the use of a seminary of learning; and 1,620 acres at the junction of the Cahawba and

Alabama rivers where the seat of government was to be laid out.

Among the men elected to the convention were some who had had experience in public affairs of the states from which they came, including three former congressmen and two supreme court judges from North Carolina.[8] Nor was it considered incongruous that Sam Dale, the most notable pioneer and Indian fighter of the Alabama country, should sit among them. On the whole, the members seem to have been selected quietly and with the intention of securing the best available men. From among their number six governors, six state supreme court judges, and six United States senators were later selected.[9]

The convention assembled at Huntsville on July 5, 1819, and John W. Walker was elected to preside. A committee of fifteen was instructed to draw up and submit a frame of government; no journal was kept of the proceedings of this committee. The proposed constitution was accepted by the convention with practically no amendments, so that very little is known concerning the process by which it was adopted. It was modeled largely after the Mississippi constitution, the striking feature being that it made the legislature superior to the other branches of government. The governor's veto could be over-ridden by a majority of those elected to each house of the legislature, and all state judges were elected by a joint vote of that body. These judges held office during good behavior, but could be removed on an address to the governor adopted by a two-thirds vote of the legislature. The heads of the executive departments—the Secretary of State, the Treasurer and Comptroller, the Attorney General—were elected by a joint vote of the General Assembly, it being the duty of the first of these to keep a record of the acts of the governor and to lay the same before the Assembly.

The social and political temper of the convention may be judged from the constitutional provisions in regard to suffrage and representation. All white, adult males who were citizens of the United States and who had resided for a year in the state were given the right to vote. Representation, both in the Senate and in the House, was to be apportioned according to the white population; nor was there any property qualification for representatives. On the question of slavery, the legislature was given no power to emancipate slaves without the consent of their owners, but owners might secure the emancipation of their slaves, and the legislature was given power to prohibit the introduction of Negroes for sale. (For further discussion of the provisions on slavery see pages 77, 165-169.)

The constitution provided that a state bank might be established with as many branches as the legislature might direct, but no branch was to be established nor bank charter renewed except by a two-thirds vote of each legislative house, nor could more than one branch be established or bank charter be renewed at any one session of the General Assembly. (See figure 5.) It was also provided that the banks already existing might become branches of the state bank by agreement between them and the assembly, in which case, however, they were bound by the same rules as applied to other branches. And in all such banks and branches, it was necessary that two-fifths of the stock and a proportional representation in the directory be reserved to the state.[11]

It was provided that the first session of the General Assembly should meet at Huntsville, and after that it was to meet at Cahawba until 1825. The first session which should meet in that year would have power, without the consent of the governor, to designate a permanent seat of government, but if this were not done, the seat was to remain permanently at Cahawba.

The General Assembly might, by a two-thirds vote of each House, propose amendments to the constitution. These had to be published three months before the next general election of representatives; and if a majority of votes were cast in favor of an amendment, the next session of the assembly might incorporate it into the constitution by a two-thirds vote of each house. Thus the initiative as well as the final action in changing the constitution was in the hands of the legislature.

This instrument of government, judged by the standards of the time, was liberal. In the older states, restricted suffrage, dis-

FIGURE 5: Vote on establishment of branch banks

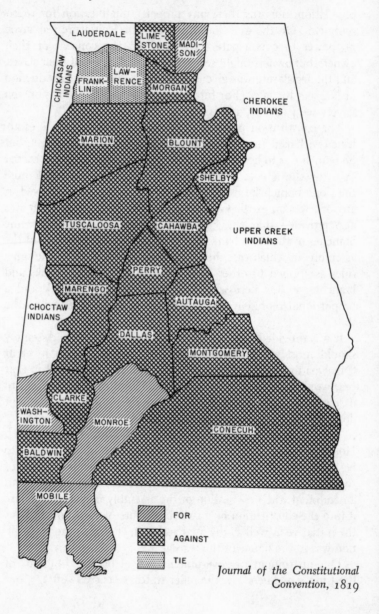

Journal of the Constitutional Convention, 1819

crimination against religious denominations, unequal representation, and imprisonment for debt, were still common. In Alabama, imprisonment for debt was to be forbidden, slaves were to be treated as liberally as circumstances seemed to warrant, and no interest nor section was to be given special weight in the councils of the state. It is significant that the slaveholder was given no advantage over the non-slaveholder in the matter of suffrage and representation.

All this looks like pioneer democracy as it came to be understood under Andrew Jackson. But there was a difference. Manhood suffrage meant a government by the people, but once they had voted, their power passed to a remarkable degree into the hands of their representatives. The legislature controlled the executive and the judiciary and dominated in the matter of constitutional amendment. Pure Jacksonian democracy would not have consented to a bench elected by the legislature and holding office during good behavior. Though the government was framed along liberal lines, the conservative element was strongly evident. Instead of reserving as much power as possible to the hands of the people, power was placed in the hands of those chosen to represent the people.

The convention made provisions for the election of representatives and officials under the new government, and the constitution went into effect without being submitted to the people.[12] It served Alabama until the War of Secession with only three amendments.

In the selection of officials, the contest for the governorship and the question of the federal judgeship are of especial interest in that they foreshadow political alignments that were of more than temporary importance. Bibb, the territorial governor, was at first the only candidate for the governorship. Later Marmaduke Williams of Tuscaloosa decided to run against him. Bibb lived in the southern section of Alabama and his choice of Cahawba as the seat of government had provoked strong opposition in the northern section.[13] Of course, there was no chance of locating the capital in the Tennessee Valley, but Tuscaloosa was accessible to that section by way of the Jones Valley route. This town, though within a few miles of the Mississippi line, was also easily accessible to the southern part of Alabama, because of its situation on navigable water and on the thoroughfare between the two sections of the state. The Tennessee Valley region united with the Black Warrior and upper Tombigbee regions in support of Tuscaloosa as the logical seat of government, and Williams was fitted to express this sentiment. Bibb was the stronger candidate, however, and his influence with the national government would probably prove of much use to the new state. With the exception of two counties in the Tennessee Valley which Bibb carried, the line which separates the waters of the Black Warrior and Tombigbee from the waters of the Alabama was the line which separated the conservative supporters of Bibb from those of Williams.[14] The election was won by Bibb. (See figure 6.)

The first General Assembly of the state met at Huntsville in October, and one of its most important duties was to elect the two United States senators. There was an understanding that one was to come from the South and one from the North, with each section ready to vote for the candidate put forward by the other. The choice of the Tennessee Valley easily fell upon John W. Walker; nor did it take the Alabama and Tombigbee section long to decide on William R. King.[15] King had represented North Carolina in Congress as a "War Hawk" during those exciting days preceding the War of 1812. He had later served as secretary of legislation to William Pinckney at Naples and St. Petersburg, and a long political career now awaited him in Alabama.[16]

Because of the agreement between the two sections, the choice of the senators passed off quietly enough in the legislature, but there was commotion below the surface. Charles Tait, after his valuable services to Alabama in the United States Senate, had returned to private life and had taken up residence in the southern part of the new state. It was not natural that he should be passed over in the matter of political preferment, and he had at least one friend who did not intend that he should be overlooked—William H. Crawford, Secretary of the Treasury. Crawford and Tait

FIGURE 6: Vote for governor, 1819

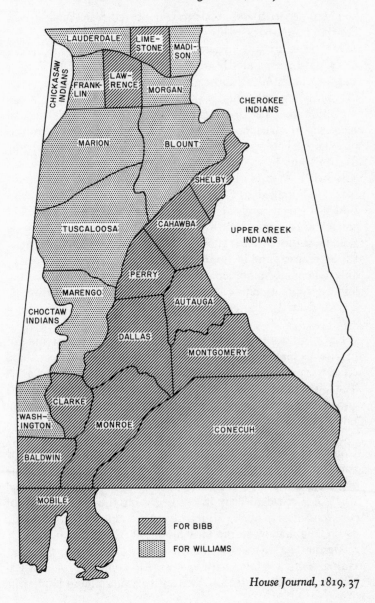

LAUDERDALE | LIMESTONE | MADISON
CHICKASAW INDIANS
FRANKLIN | LAWRENCE | MORGAN
CHEROKEE INDIANS
MARION | BLOUNT
SHELBY
TUSCALOOSA | CAHAWBA
UPPER CREEK INDIANS
PERRY
MARENGO | AUTAUGA
CHOCTAW INDIANS
DALLAS
MONTGOMERY
CLARKE
WASHINGTON | MONROE | CONECUH
BALDWIN
MOBILE

FOR BIBB
FOR WILLIAMS

House Journal, 1819, 37

had become fast friends while teaching together in Augusta, and they later came to be political allies.

The Secretary was anxious for Tait to be sent to the Senate from Alabama,[17] and Tait would not have objected. But Walker and his friends in the north could not further this ambition, for the south was choosing its own candidate, and it chose King. Tait indicated that his second choice would be for the federal judgeship in Alabama,[18] but there was another candidate for this place also. Toulmin had been federal judge for the Alabama Territory and it was natural that he should expect to retain his place when Alabama became a state. William Crawford of Alabama had applied to Governor Bibb for the appointment, and Bibb had recommended him to the Secretary of the Treasury; but when the Alabama Crawford heard that Tait wanted the position, he withdrew his request.[19] Bibb then recommended Tait to the Secretary,[20] and by this time Walker was in Washington and able to help his friend. He went to the President with the matter, and the appointment was easily put through, Monroe answering a letter from Toulmin to the effect that he could do nothing for him.[21]

Crawford was in control of the patronage of Alabama and put his friends into office wherever he could. He even offered a land office receivership to King in order to get him out of the way of Tait's senatorial ambitions. This situation naturally aroused the antagonism of those who sought office in vain, and tended to unite all elements against the men from Georgia who were strongest numerically in the neighborhood of Montgomery County, but who constituted a powerful minority in Huntsville and other towns. Denunciation of the "Georgia faction" became common, and the Georgia men, seeing the danger in this, did what they could to allay it, even securing the appointment of some outsiders to office.[22] But here was a political situation which cast a long shadow on the early history of Alabama.

During the first session of the General Assembly, there occurred another event which will serve to complete the political picture of Alabama in 1819. General Jackson came to Huntsville with his horses to take part in some racing. Such an occasion could not be passed over in silence and the legislature took the opportunity to celebrate.[23] A resolution admitting the General within the bar of both houses was passed, and another approving his course in the Seminole War was introduced. The second resolution read:

> And be it further resolved that this General Assembly do highly disapprove of the late attempt made by some members of the Congress of the United States at the last session to censure the military course of this inestimable officer from motives (as we believe) other than patriotic.

It was carried in the House by a majority of twenty-seven to twenty-one, five counties voting in favor of it and six splitting their votes equally.[24] (See figure 7.)

On the surface, the action taken by the General Assembly does not appear to be significant. But James G. Birney, who lived in Huntsville in the days before he became a leader of abolitionists and who was not a member of the Assembly, signed his political death warrant in Alabama by opposing the Jackson resolution.[25] The same is true of most of the others who took a similar stand. Jacksonism had not been an issue when the Assembly was elected and many got seats whose opinions would have debarred them at a later time.

But such men as Birney had strong company. Governor Bibb wrote to Tait concerning Jackson's attack on Pensacola in the Seminole War:

> Government has done right respecting the occupation of Florida, except in apologies for Genl. Jackson. In that they have erred (according to my judgment) most egregiously. They will gain nothing by it with his friends, and lose much with the thinking part of the nation. Not a moment should have been lost in arresting the Genl. and thereby showing a just regard to the preservation of our constitution. No man should be permitted in a free country to usurp the whole powers of the whole government and to thwart with contempt all authority except that of his own will.[26]

FIGURE 7: Vote to disapprove censuring of Jackson, 1819

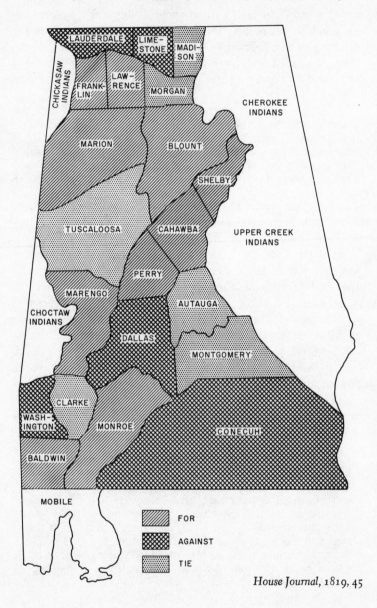

Walker showed a different spirit. He wrote to Tait:

> I fear we think too much alike about some things touching the
> Seminole War. I would to God they were undone. He [Jack-
> son] is a great man with great defects. One cannot help loving
> or blaming him. But I follow your exemplary course—and per-
> haps go further: when I cannot praise I try to be silent.[27]

As for the opinion of the more eminent friends of these Alabama leaders, Crawford expressed his sentiments very clearly in
a letter to Governor David Holmes, of the Mississippi Territory,
in 1818:

> Persons so regardless of our laws as those engaged in the expedi-
> tion against Pensacola deserve their severest penalties, and you
> may rely upon my exertions to bring them to punishment.[28]

Calhoun, Crawford's colleague in the Cabinet as Secretary of
War, wrote to Tait palliating the conduct of Jackson and uphold-
ing the course of the Administration.[29] But there was evidently
trouble ahead in Alabama for those who did not uphold "The
General."

CHAPTER SIX

The Public Lands

WHEN THE WAR OF 1812 AND THE BLOCKADE OF the coast cut off the export of cotton to British markets, the price fell in America while it rose in England. With the return of peace, this condition was reversed. English mills bought heavily to make up for lost time, and the price went up with a bound, averaging nearly thirty cents a pound for 1816. The situation would hardly have been expected to last, and the next year the market fell off to an average of about twenty-seven cents a pound. At these figures the production of the staple was distinctly profitable, and planters began to move in large numbers to the new lands in Alabama. But 1818 proved to be an exceptional year. Instead of continuing to fall off, the price of cotton rose to the unprecedented average of about thirty-four cents a pound. A rush to the western lands resulted and prices ranging from $50 to $100 an acre were paid for farms lying in a virgin wilderness.[1]

The monetary situation of the country favored this spirit of speculation. There had been a general suspension of specie payments during the War and the currency of the country had fallen into great disorder. Many of the bank notes that circulated were of uncertain value and much inconvenience was caused by their use. Largely in order to remedy this state of affairs, the second Bank of the United States was chartered in 1816 and was to go into operation early in 1817. A resolution was passed that the government would receive only specie-paying paper after February 20. In order to effect resumption, the banks of issue had to cut down their circulation, but the object was accomplished, and by February specie payment had been restored.[2]

The reduction in the number of notes in circulation which accompanied the resumption of specie payments would have tended to retard speculation under ordinary circumstances; but the temptation of the cotton lands in the West was too great to be denied, and means were found to overcome the difficulty. In the first place, the management of the new Bank of the United States was reckless, and its notes were turned loose largely in the South[3] to be invested by the speculators. But more important than this, about seventy local banks were founded in Tennessee and Kentucky in 1818.[4] These institutions had troubled careers, but their notes remained good long enough to make the first payment on government lands.

Still another resource was open to many of those who wished to purchase land in Alabama. The $5,000,000 in scrip which had been issued to the Yazoo claimants was redeemable only in payments for lands in the Georgia cession; and since no new Indian cessions had been obtained within Mississippi, the first chance afforded the Yazoo men for redeeming their scrip was at the Alabama sales of 1817 and 1818. The greater part of it was turned in at this time to make the first payments on purchases, and it added much to the frenzy of speculation.

Land sales during this period were made under the act of 1800, as extended and amended in 1803 and 1804.[6] It was provided that the public domain should be surveyed by marking it off into townships six miles square, and the townships subdivided into thirty-six square miles or sections. A quarter-section, or 160 acres, was the smallest tract which could be sold.

Having been surveyed, the land was advertised for sale at public auctions which were held at the offices established in the various land districts. Tracts were sold to the highest bidder, and those remaining unsold might be entered privately at the minimum price of $2.00 an acre. In either case, one-fourth of the purchase money had to be paid at the time of the sale, and the remaining three-fourths in annual installments of one-fourth each.

The surveys in the Creek cession were begun in 1816,[7] and speculators at once began making investigations. (See figure 8.) A. P. Hayne made a tour of the lands to be put on the market and wrote to Andrew Jackson giving a favorable account of the rich river and prairie tracts.[8] Jackson wrote to a friend in Washington to inquire as to the price of the Yazoo scrip and found that it had risen from $40 to $68.[9] Companies were formed for participation at the auctions, and Hayne wrote that "speculation in land is superior to Law or Physic."[10]

The first sale took place at Milledgeville, Georgia, in August, 1817, and comprised a tract lying along the headwaters of the Alabama River in the neighborhood of the present city of Montgomery.[11] Only the best river bottom tracts were disposed of at this time, and these were taken up by speculators from various places. The men who had moved into the region were generally too poor to make their way to the place of sale, and they had little hope of being able to compete with the wealthier purchasers.[12] Sales during this year amounted to nearly $800,000, and the new tracts in the same region which were offered in 1818 brought the sales of that year up to nearly $1,000,000.[13]

Almost nothing but river bottom lands were sold at Milledgeville during these two years,[14] and there were few actual settlers among the purchasers.

The most coveted acreage disposed of at this time lay within a wide bend of the Alabama River and upon a bluff which formed the opposite bank. The soil in the bend was of the best quality, and the bluff afforded an excellent site for a town. Members of the Bibb family were anxious to purchase here, and so was A. P. Hayne, who wrote to Jackson concerning the matter.[15] A land company, of which William Wyatt Bibb was a member, secured the tracts, and the town of Montgomery was founded upon the bluff in 1819.[16]

Large as these sales were, they were small in comparison with those which were held in Huntsville in 1818. All the lands lying

FIGURE 8: Indian cessions in Alabama

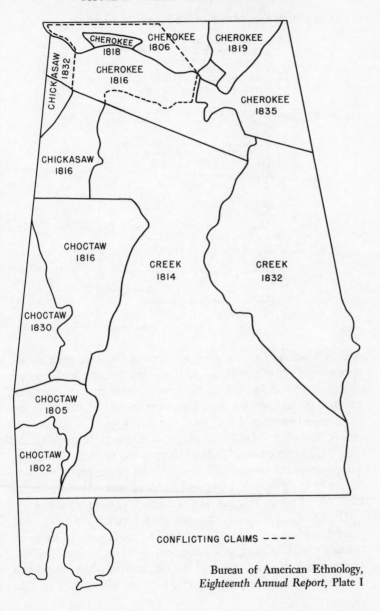

CONFLICTING CLAIMS ----

Bureau of American Ethnology,
Eighteenth Annual Report, Plate I

FIGURE 9: Value of lands sold in Alabama

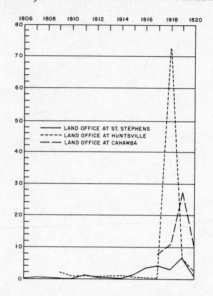

American State Papers, Lands, V, 384-385

west of Madison County, on both sides of the Tennessee River, were offered for sale in that year,[17] and the amount sold reached a value of $7,000,000. Out of the sum of about $1,500,000 which was paid down upon the purchases, over $1,000,000 was in Yazoo scrip, or "Mississippi stock," as it was called.[18]

A speculating company, composed of men from Virginia, Georgia, Kentucky, and Madison County was formed. Prominent Tennesseans bid against this combine and prices were run up to figures ranging between $50 and $100 an acre. Average cotton land sold at prices between $20 and $30.[19] (See figure 9.)

The excitement caused by the sales was nation-wide. Men came from every part of the country to participate in them. A company was formed in Charleston, South Carolina, for the purpose of buying acreage in Alabama, and Stephen Elliott was sent out to make the purchases.[20] Much swindling went on during the sales. A company of speculators would combine, and, by a show of force, intimidate their competitors and bid off large tracts of desirable land at low prices. They would then sell out at a considerable gain to those who had not been able to compete with them. It is stated on good authority that one such association of swindlers cleared $1,980 each on a transaction of this kind.[21] The situation became so notorious that the government authorized its agents to bid against the combination when they thought it advisable.[22]

No such extent of fine lands was ever again offered for sale in Alabama during a single year, but in 1819 large areas along the Alabama River below Montgomery County were put on the market. The land office for this district had now been moved from Milledgeville to Cahawba, and the sales here amounted to nearly $3,000,000 during the year.

By the time the credit system of sales was abolished in 1820, Alabama had, in all, amassed a land debt of $11,000,000, or more than half the total for the entire country.[23] And in the meantime the price of cotton had gone down to eighteen cents; the country was in the throes of commercial depression; and the prospect of paying for the lands which had been bought at abnormal prices became almost hopeless.

Such a state of affairs prompted Congress to discontinue the policy of credit sales. In 1820 it was provided that half quarter-sections might be sold; that the minimum price should be $1.25 an acre; and that all payments should be in cash. The system of public auctions followed by private entry was continued.[24]

But something had to be done for those who had already fallen into debt beyond hope of recovery, and this problem was attacked in 1821. It was provided that land which had been purchased but not completely paid for might be relinquished and the sum paid on it applied on the balance due for lands which were retained. In addition to this, the balance due on lands retained was to be reduced by 37½ percent, and an extension of credit was to be granted.[25] Large numbers took advantage of this act, and within a year the land debt of Alabama was reduced by half. Those who did not take advantage of it were later given a chance to do so, and by 1825 the debt had been decreased to $3,677,285.[26]

Yet the consequences of the speculation of 1818 and 1819 were not so easily overcome. The men who relinquished their land under the act of 1821 did not consider that they were giving up their right to it. They continued to live upon and cultivate it, and expected to be able to buy it back some day under favorable arrangements which they looked to Congress to make. Thus the community was injured by the presence of a large number of farmers who were mere tenants by common consent. The unsettled condition of such men was disturbing to the whole system of rural economy. By 1828 about 3,250,000 out of the 24,000,000 acres of public lands in Alabama were sold, and nearly half as much had been relinquished.[27] The extent of the evil can be imagined.

In the natural course of events, the relinquished lands would be put on the market again at auction sale, and here the relinquisher would have to compete with all comers in bids for fields that he had owned and cleared and still cultivated. The spirit of the community was in sympathy with the relinquisher. It would hardly have been considered honorable to bid against him for lands which were looked on as his by natural right. However, there were many sharpers who made it a business to prey upon those who had made improvements upon lands to which they did not have title. It was their practice to go to the interested party and threaten to bid against him unless he made terms. An agreement was generally reached, and the settler had to pay the sharper about as much as he paid the government for his lands.[28]

The same situation was faced by others in addition to the relinquishers. The more desirable areas in the state, accessible to river communication, were the first to be surveyed and sold. Later on, the more inaccessible areas were put on the market. Where men of small means had come into Alabama and settled upon desirable lands in the river regions, they were frequently unable to hold them when they were put up for sale at auction. It became necessary for these people to move out into the back country and start all over again, but the auctioneer in time came to them in their newer homes. Here, however, the situation was different. The speculative period was over after 1819 and lands would no longer bring abnormally high prices. The back country tracts, being relatively inaccessible, would not command prices much above the statutory minimum, even though they were fertile, nor would a man's neighbor bid against him for lands which he had improved. Consequently, the settler in the less accessible districts would normally have been able to buy his improved land at a price close to $1.25 an acre had not the sharper attacked him in the same manner in which he attacked the relinquisher.[29] Land offices were established in Tuscaloosa and Conecuh counties in 1820, and men who had not yet been called upon to prove their titles began to fear that they would lose their homes in the competition of the sales. There is on record the case of a preacher in Conecuh County who was forced by swindlers to pay $37.50 an acre for the privilege of buying his lands without competition, but the fraud became known to the government, the sale was canceled, and the parson was able to buy in his land at the minimum price.[30] Public auctions were more than once suspended because of the operation of swindlers.

In order to obviate such difficulties, it was strongly advocated in Alabama that the unsold lands be divided into classes and that each class be given a price according to its grade. Actual settlers were to be allowed to enter their lands at the fixed prices and thus be assured in the tenure of their fields and their homes. This plan was especially urged in regard to the relinquished lands, and Alabama's representatives in Washington worked for the adoption of the proposal, but nothing came of their efforts.[31] There was adopted, instead, an act which permitted those who had relinquished or forfeited lands to repurchase them at a reduction of 37½ percent on the original price.[32] This did not remedy the situation, and the auction continued to harass the settlers.

CHAPTER SEVEN

Agriculture

BY 1820 ALABAMA HAD ATTRACTED A POPULATION of over 125,000, black and white, and of these the slaves made up 31 percent. This was about the same proportion which had existed between the races in 1816 when Alabama was still a part of the Mississippi Territory and contained but two widely-separated settlements. By 1830 the population had swelled beyond 300,000 and the percent of slaves had gradually risen from 31 to 38. Thus during this period of rapid immigration and the planting of the cotton kingdom in the lower South, there were about two white men coming in for every slave that entered. If the whites averaged five to the family and the slaves ten to the master, only one family in four could have been of the slaveholding class.[1] (See figures 10, 11, and 12.)

During this early period the population was widely spread over the face of the country, but there was a striking segregation of the slave population into certain districts. In 1830 there was but one county in the state, Madison, with over 16,000 population, and only seven of the most barren had less than 4,000. The counties which attracted the heaviest population were those of the Tennessee Valley and those of the region of clay ridges skirting the hilly district of the northeastern part of the state.

On the other hand, the slave population was very largely confined to the counties of the Tennessee Valley and to those lying along the navigable portions of the Alabama and Tombigbee

FIGURE 10: Slave population, 1818

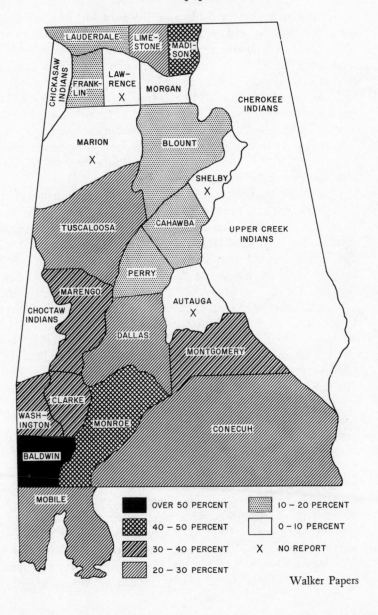

Walker Papers

rivers. The river bottom lands were the most highly prized by
the cotton planters because of their great fertility, but these were
of limited extent, and it was necessary to resort to the ridge lands
lying along the courses of the rivers. The prairie region, or Black
Belt, which later came to be so highly esteemed for cotton culture, was avoided by the planters before 1830 because they had
not learned how to master the difficulties of the sticky soil.[2] In se-
lecting his site, the planter had to consider communications as
well as fertility of soil, and continuity of fields also counted for
something. These factors combined to make the river valleys the
slave sections of the state before 1830.

How soon cotton culture came to be an established industry in
Alabama cannot be stated with accuracy. The staple is said to
have been produced to some extent as early as 1772,[3] and by 1807
it had come largely to supplant indigo in the agriculture of the
Tombigbee region.[4] It is fairly clear that the Georgians who
came to Madison County in 1809 came for the purpose of planting cotton, and it is stated that the crop of that county in 1816
amounted to 10,000 bales.[5] Certainly by the time of the great
immigration in 1817 and 1818 the economic prospects of Alabama must have been clear to practically all who entered. Yet
William Darby, in his *Emigrant's Guide* of 1818, states that extensive vineyards would be planted upon the dry slopes of the
Alabama if ever anywhere in the United States, and that the
olive would find a congenial soil upon the banks of the Alabama,
Cahawba, Coosa, and Tallapoosa rivers.[6] That this view was seriously entertained at that time is proven by the attempt of the
ill-fated colony of Napoleonic refugees to bring forth the grapes
and olives of southern France on the banks of the Tombigbee in
1817.[7] It was probably their failure which precluded further
earnest attempts along that line, but when cotton prospects were
gloomy, there were those who urged experiments with other
crops. Grapes, sugar cane, and small grain were all suggested at
different times,[8] and limited experiments were made with each.
Yet Alabama was to have but two predominant systems of agriculture: that of the planter who raised cotton, with corn as his

FIGURE 11: Slave population, 1824

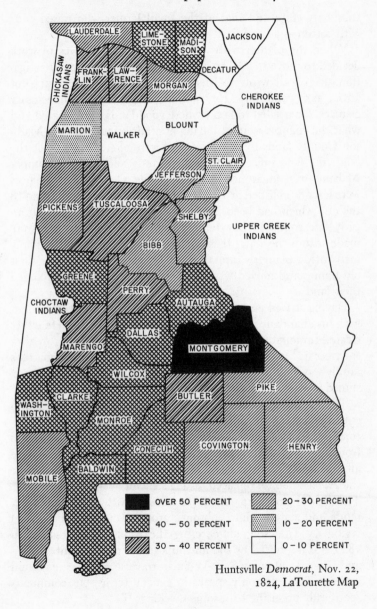

Huntsville *Democrat*, Nov. 22,
1824, LaTourette Map

subsidiary crop; and that of the small farmer who raised corn with cotton as a subsidiary.

When the planter with money to invest and slaves to work decided to move to Alabama, he often made a tour of investigation, or at least wrote to friends in the new country asking for advice as to conditions. He could not afford to take unnecessary chances. He needed to know where good lands were located and what the chances were of buying at a fair price. The first Madison County lands to be disposed of were offered for sale at the Nashville land office, and the first lands sold along the upper Alabama were auctioned at Milledgeville, Georgia. Land offices were later established at Huntsville and Cahawba, in addition to the one which had been put in operation at St. Stephens at an early date, so that all but the very first sales in these districts were made within the state. It is unreasonable to suppose that many men with a planter's capital at stake would have sold out their old homes and moved westward without first having purchased their land.

Having arrived upon his new estate, it did not take the planter, with his abundance of labor, long to establish himself. He either cleared some ground immediately or planted the first crop after the trees had been deadened by girdling. A house for the master's family was built of logs, and the routine of plantation life was resumed as well as the crude conditions permitted.[9]

The log house, so typical of a frontier community, was not an ephemeral thing. It remained the standard of domestic architecture in the more isolated sections and was sometimes adhered to from inertia or sentimental reasons by men who could easily have afforded more modern quarters. It was not long, however, before the average planter replaced his log structure with one of boards. The typical Southern "mansion house," with its generous veranda and stately white columns, arose throughout the cotton region. A. Hodgson, on entering the Montgomery district in 1820, was impressed by the fine appearance of the plantations,[10] and Duke Bernhard of Saxe-Weimar, traversing the same ground six years later, not only speaks in general terms, but comments specifically upon the handsome dwellings.[11]

FIGURE 12: Slave population, 1830

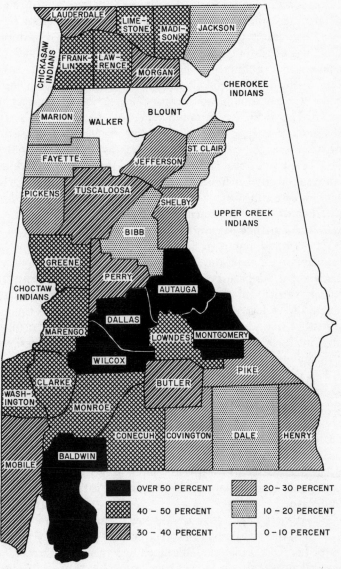

LAUDERDALE
LIME-STONE
MADI-SON
JACKSON
CHICKASAW INDIANS
FRANK-LIN
LAW-RENCE
MORGAN
CHEROKEE INDIANS
MARION
WALKER
BLOUNT
FAYETTE
JEFFERSON
ST. CLAIR
PICKENS
TUSCALOOSA
SHELBY
UPPER CREEK INDIANS
BIBB
GREENE
PERRY
AUTAUGA
CHOCTAW INDIANS
DALLAS
MARENGO
LOWNDES
MONTGOMERY
WILCOX
PIKE
CLARKE
BUTLER
WASH-INGTON
MONROE
CONECUH
COVINGTON
DALE
HENRY
MOBILE
BALDWIN

OVER 50 PERCENT
40 – 50 PERCENT
30 – 40 PERCENT
20 – 30 PERCENT
10 – 20 PERCENT
0 – 10 PERCENT

U.S. Census, 1830

In general appearance, the homes of the Southwestern planters resembled those which Thomas Jefferson's classical revival had inspired in Virginia. They were white, two-storied buildings of classical proportions, with broad verandas and tall columns. But a different spirit showed itself in plan and execution. Instead of a well-knit structure with architectural finish, there was a rambling house with a suggestion of unnecessary space. The difference, it would seem, was due primarily to the shaping influence of the log cabin. The simple cabin, consisting of two rooms joined by a wide "breeze-way," which had only a floor below and a roof above, accustomed the pioneer to architecture embodying generous open-air passages. The planter started his new career in such a house, but sometimes amplified it into a dwelling of from four to eight rooms, keeping to the same materials and method of construction throughout. Finally, when he built his frame house, he followed the old lines of internal arrangement. Crossing the veranda with its tall columns, one entered a spacious hallway which served no particular purpose, but merely carried out the idea of the open passage between the rooms of the log cabin. The large rooms which flanked the hall on either side were almost invariably square and regular in design, just as they must have been had they been built of logs. And the plan upstairs was the same as below.[12]

But the plantation was much more than a house and lands. Being, if it chose to be, largely independent of the outside world for its daily supplies, it was a community in itself. Grouped about the mansion were the barns, the smokehouse where pork was cured, the cotton gin and press, and quarters for the slaves. Places were frequently advertised for sale in the early newspapers, and such advertisements furnish an interesting description of the equipment of a plantation in houses, barns, cattle, mules, swine, and slaves.[13]

Slaves were rated, according to their fitness, full, three-quarters, half, and quarter hands, and given tasks accordingly. Adding these fractions, a planter determined how many "full hands," or equivalents, made up his working force. A census of Madison

County for 1819 gives nearly twelve acres of cleared land for every full hand,[14] and other evidence makes it clear that each hand rated at full work was expected to cultivate five or six acres of cotton and an equal area in corn.[15]

There were several reasons for devoting the land in nearly equal parts to cotton and corn. A gang of hands could plant more cotton than they could possibly pick, so that a part of their time had to be devoted to some other crop, and corn had a particular place in the economy of the plantation. The weekly allowance of bread-stuff to the slave was a peck of meal, and this, together with his allowance of pork—the supply of which was also dependent on the corn crop—made up the regular fare of the working force. The slaves usually had garden plots of their own, and could sometimes add fish or game to their diet by hunting or fishing in spare time. The watermelon and the 'possum were favorites then as now, but corn and pork made up the regular fare throughout the year.[16]

Clothing was issued twice yearly—in the spring and in the fall. Suits of osnaburg, or coarse cotton clothing, were provided for the summer, and "plains," or coarse woolen stuff for the winter. Hats, shoes, and blankets completed the list of articles which had to be furnished by the master. Medical attention was provided for the sick and nurseries for the children of mothers who went to the field. Altogether, the maintenance of a slave for a year, including his food allowance, his clothing, blankets, and medical attention, cost between $20 and $25.[17]

Judicious farming required that the master produce all his own corn and pork, but, especially when the price of cotton was high, he was likely to increase his crop of the staple and buy corn in the market.[18] This kind of speculative planting was not only bad from an economic point of view, but tended to overwork the slaves during the picking season. For the small farmer, excessive cotton planting meant that his family was put on short rations.[19] But such practices as this seem to have been common during the early, speculative period of the industry in the state. Though periods of low prices operated to check this over-planting of cotton, it is certainly true that during the early 'twenties, a large quantity of corn and pork was imported from other states by the planters, and many complaints were made about it by the agricultural critics.

There seems to have been little difference between the methods employed in the culture of cotton and of corn, but cotton received more attention. The agricultural year began about the middle of February, when the first plowing could be done. All the old cotton and corn stalks were gathered and burned, and the ground was bedded up by running one furrow and then lapping several others upon it. This process was called "listing."

The cotton was planted during March by running a drill down the center of the beds and sowing the cotton seed rather thickly in the drill. The seeds were covered by attaching a board with a concave surface to a plow and drawing it along the crest of the bed. When the young cotton was well above the ground, the stand was thinned with a hoe, leaving only two stalks in one place. Later, another thinning reduced the stand to a single stalk in a place. The distance between the beds and between the stalks in the bed varied according to the fertility of the soil or the caprice of the planter. Three and a half feet between beds and eight inches between stalks was given as a fair average for the Tennessee Valley.[20]

Frequent cultivation was necessary in order to keep down the grass and weeds, and this was done partly by the plow and partly by the hoe. Favorable comments made by travelers into the cotton region indicated that crops were usually kept in very good condition. The bolls began to open the latter part of August, but they fruited gradually, and had to be picked often in order to prevent damage to the fibre. This was the busiest time of the year and all available help was called in. The picking went on steadily through the fall months and well into the winter. Sometimes a part of the crop was still in the field and had to be destroyed when the time for spring plowing arrived.[21]

Ginning was also a slow process compared with modern methods. Every planter of any importance had his own gin-house where his staple was prepared for the market. If properly prepared, the cotton had to be carefully picked over by hand for the removal of trash and yellow flakes before it went to the gin; and after coming from the machine, it always had in it particles of seed and other foreign matter which had to be removed by another picking over, or moting. The ginned cotton was taken to the press where it was squeezed into bales of about 350 pounds. The gin and the press were both run by horse power, and several hands were kept busy at the work.[22]

During the decade, however, two important advances were made in the processes of preparing cotton. In 1822 "Carver's Improved Gin" was introduced in Mississippi, and its advantages were noised abroad in the agricultural papers. It was claimed that the new machine did not tear the fibre while removing it from the seed, and that the quality of the staple was thereby much improved. James Jackson and General John Coffee brought the new gin into the Tennessee Valley, and the cotton which they turned out with it was said to be of unusual quality.[23] In 1824 the first supply of these machines was received at Mobile.[24]

At about the same time there was contrived and introduced in Mississippi an apparatus for moting the cotton as it came from the gin. In Whitney's gin the cotton fibre was removed from the seed by means of revolving saw-teeth, and revolving brushes removed the fibre from the saws. The arms of the revolving brushes were now supplied with fans which blew the issuing cotton through a horizontal wooden flue with a latticed bottom. As the lint passed through the flue, the particles of foreign matter dropped through the grating into a trough below. Thus a large part of the labor of moting was dispensed with.[25]

The ginning and baling of cotton was a matter of great importance because the market value of the staple depended largely upon its freedom from flaws and foreign matter. Many complaints were made as to the carelessness with which the Alabama planters handled their product. It was stated that though the staple of the Alabama cotton was as good as that of any upland variety, it brought a lower price than that of either Georgia or Louisiana because of the indifferent way in which it was ginned and handled.[26] The truth of this statement is hard to judge. Louisiana and Mississippi cotton consistently brought a higher price than that of Alabama. That of South Alabama and Georgia stood on a fairly equal footing, while that of Tennessee and North Alabama usually brought the lowest price. The adaptability of climate and soil to the cotton crop in these several localities was undoubtedly the prime factor in these distinctions, but it is quite likely that there was also a difference in agricultural methods. As far as Alabama is concerned, the people who moved into the southern part of the state came chiefly from sections in Georgia and South Carolina where the planting of cotton was already familiar and well-established. Those who moved into the Tennessee Valley came in greater numbers from Tennessee, Virginia, and North Carolina, where cotton had never been of importance.

Alabama writers, and especially those in the Tennessee Valley, often complained that the various methods in use indicated that no scientific basis of field-management had been established. The greatest bone of contention was the distance that should be allowed between the beds and between the stalks in the beds. There was also much variety in the use of fertilizer. Many used stable manure, and some employed cotton seed, the latter sometimes mixed with leaf mold or other material and allowed to stand in great piles until spring, when the mixture was strewn in the drills. Yet there can be little doubt that the worth of cotton seed as fertilizer was generally overlooked and the valuable material thrown away.[27]

The greatest advance that was made during the decade in the culture of cotton was the introduction of the "Mexican" variety of seed. This produced larger pods which opened wider than the old variety and allowed the fibre to hang from the bolls, making the picking an easier process than it had been previously. Industrious hands were now able to pick 200 pounds a day, whereas 100 had formerly been a good average.[28]

The planting of a localized staple such as cotton was a more speculative industry than was the raising of the more widespread crops. Since the South furnished the world with most of its cotton, a bountiful crop in that section, not being offset to any great extent by differing conditions in other places, would depress the price to the full extent of the local over-production. Likewise, a short crop in the South meant a shortage of cotton for the world, and a high price which would spend its whole buoyant force upon the industry of a few states. And the planters were the most helpless of people in the matter of adjusting themselves to the varying economic conditions. Once a man had established himself as a slaveholder in the lower South, he found it hard to vary his agricultural system.[29] He could not diminish his crop much below the normal, for his slaves were efficient only when worked according to the usual routine; nor were there any facilities for marketing other crops.

It was the high price of cotton during the years following the close of the second war with England which gave Alabama her

FIGURE 13: Average yearly price of middling upland cotton

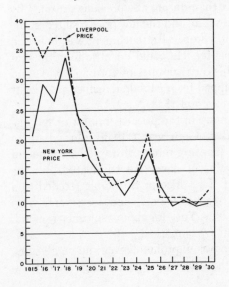

J. L. Watkins, *Production and Price of Cotton*, U.S. Department of Agriculture Miscellaneous Bulletins, No. 9, 8-9, 1895

FIGURE 14: Average valuation of slaves in Mobile

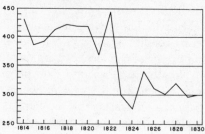

James D. D. DeBow, *Industrial Resources* . . . , II
(New Orleans, 1853), 79

first great influx of population. It will be recalled that it was in 1818 that land sales in Alabama reached their zenith. But cotton fell from thirty-four to twenty-four cents the next year; to seventeen cents in 1820; to fourteen in 1821; and in 1823 it reached bottom at about eleven cents a pound.[30] (See figure 13.) During these years of falling prices, the value of slaves declined steadily[31] (see figure 14), though there was more land cultivated in the Tennessee Valley in 1821 than during any previous season.[32] By 1823 discouragement had set in, and the low price resulted in the planting of a smaller cotton crop.[33] Retrenchment was, however, a hard matter for the planter. He could do little more in that direction than raise all his own supplies of corn and pork, and the amount of cotton shipped from Mobile remained practically stationary during 1822, 1823, and 1824.[34]

In 1825 there came a jump in the price as a result of speculation in the British market. Corn was actually plowed up in Alabama for the sake of planting more cotton;[35] the volume of the crop rose, and the value of slaves was stimulated. But the optimism was short-lived. The price of the staple receded to a lower level than it had reached before, and for several years thereafter cotton sold in New York for about ten cents a pound. The depression in Alabama was marked.

Complaints that cotton was unprofitable went up on all sides, and the need for diversification was urged. The prevalent un-

scientific methods of planting were condemned, and a widespread agitation for agricultural societies set in.[36] The governor's
message of 1826 urged diversification and suggested a standing
committee to consider the agricultural problems of the state[37]
So great had been the over-planting of cotton in 1825 that the
Alabama Journal, on September 6, 1826, proposed a special
meeting of the General Assembly to afford relief in view of the
impending scarcity of provisions. Yet there was only a temporary
decrease in the amount of cotton that went out from Mobile.

The average yearly production of cotton for a slave was, during these years, about 1,000 pounds, ginned.[38] This, at ten cents
a pound, would be worth $100, and since the maintenance of a
slave cost approximately $25 a year in money and provisions,
there remained about $75 to provide for upkeep, interest, and
profits. The indications are that ten cents was the lowest price
at which cotton could be raised at this time without a loss; but
eventually the production of a slave was increased so that a
lower price became possible.

The small farmer was not dependent upon the price of cotton.
He had come into the new country in search of economic freedom rather than fortune. He sought subsistence for his family
instead of cotton lands and access to market. He did not compete for the most fertile and accessible locations because he lacked
the capital, and because it was not in his interest to do so. A
secluded nook would serve him as well or better, for he loved the
freedom of the forest, his rifle, and his axe. He built his house of
logs, cleared his corn patches, and raised his hogs. There was a
fine range for cattle in the woods, and large herds found their
own sustenance throughout most of the year.[39]

Many, perhaps most, of the small farmers had come west with
practically no property, and their farming equipment was at first
of the crudest kind. Wheat was a familiar crop to many of them,
and it was tried in Alabama, but lack of flour mills made grinding
it a difficult problem. Corn proved to be more practicable, and
grist mills were built on the streams during the first stages of
settlement. Cotton, too, soon came to be popular with the small

farmer. Though a man could not raise supplies for his own family and plant a large cotton crop at the same time, he could raise a small amount of the staple and sell it for enough to meet his financial needs. Thus, largely because of the ease of marketing it, cotton came to be the "money crop" among the farmers.[40]

Taking a general view of the state, the several regions within Alabama differed materially in their economic composition. The Tennessee Valley, to begin with, offers the most complete picture of agricultural, and hence social and political, diversity. The Georgians who established Madison County in 1808 invested extensively in land, and, being there during the phenomenal years of 1817 and 1818, their fortunes soared. By 1826 some of them owned gangs of Negroes numbering into the hundreds.[41] Moreover, among the Virginians, North Carolinians, and Georgians who purchased lands in the Valley in 1818 were men of extensive wealth. The speculative conditions under which the valley region west of Madison County was opened up served to exclude men of moderate means from securing desirable tracts. But all the northern counties contained lands lying outside the valley region, and consequently there remained many less desirable tracts which could be taken up by private entry after the auction sales were over. Tennesseeans of moderate means came down in large numbers and settled in the same counties with the wealthy planters.

This diversity of origin and station between close neighbors developed a certain antagonism which was aggravated by the commercial situation. The cotton of the Valley had to be lightered over Muscle Shoals and then floated all the way down to New Orleans before it could be marketed. To have a crop ginned and baled, and shipped in this way to merchants in New Orleans, then to cash the draft which was received in return and secure the proceeds, required months of delay and entailed reliance upon forwarding agents, brokers, and banks, which the small producer was not able to face on his own account. In order to avoid all this, he sometimes sold his cotton in the seed to local merchants who provided him with necessary supplies. Sometimes he prepared his crop for shipment and turned it over to a merchant who advanced him a certain percent of its value and paid the balance when the remittance came up from New Orleans.[42] In either case, he was likely to lose at every turn in the transaction, and this condition of commercial dependence tended to make him resentful of those with whom he was forced to do business. The political result of this situation made the Tennessee Valley a hotbed of partisan contention.

This section seems to have gone in more for quantity than quality,[43] and its cotton brought the lowest prices on the market. When a crop was disposed of to a country merchant, the staple was usually taken at a uniform price.[44] The fact that a large part of the output was sold in this way may account for the relatively careless handling in the Tennessee Valley. Picking and preparing the staple for market required great care, and negligence in these processes resulted in a trashy fibre that greatly reduced the cotton's value. Over-planting caused congestion during the picking season and naturally led to careless handling.

Over-planting also made it necessary to purchase a large part of the corn and pork supply for the Negroes, and importation of these articles into the Tennessee Valley was large. The trade was encouraged by the ease with which such products could be brought down the river from East Tennessee.

Occupying the north-central portion of the state and extending from the Tennessee Valley to the navigable waters of the Alabama and Tombigbee rivers, lay the hilly region. Here the isolated valleys were settled by men of pioneer instincts who began to come in as early as 1815. Small clearings were made and log cabins rose here and there. The woods furnished abundant game and an excellent range for cattle, while corn and hogs were relied upon as the principal food supplies. In other words, this region reproduced the characteristics which always typified the advancing frontier in this area.

Since a large majority of the inhabitants of Alabama were of the farmer rather than the planter class, and since the planters needed supplies of corn and pork which the farmers principally raised, it seems strange, at first glance, that the hilly region did not send large quantities of these products into the river valley regions. This would have been an easily accessible market for the farmers, and the planters would have had a convenient source of supply, but no such trade ever reached significant proportions. The explanation is that cotton rather than corn was the farmer's money crop. Cotton was easier to handle, and the financial return was evidently more satisfactory despite the fact that the small producer could not own his gin nor market his crop except by disposing of it to a local merchant. For the greater part of the central hilly region, Tuscaloosa, at the head of navigation on the Black Warrior, was the most convenient market after the steamboat came into general use. The road which connected Tuscaloosa with Huntsville passed through Jones Valley, in which Birmingham now stands; and along this route most of the cotton was carried to market and the supplies of coffee, sugar, and flour brought back to the farm.[45]

Though the sticky soil of the Black Belt was avoided by the planter until about 1830, there were fertile tracts of land upon the northern border of the prairie which proved attractive to the first planters who immigrated to Alabama. These areas, together with the bottom lands along the Alabama and Tombigbee rivers, constituted the cotton section of the southern part of the state. (See figure 15.)

Excepting in the prairie region, the stretches of good land here were not so extensive as in the Tennessee Valley, and the planter lived in closer relationship with the man who farmed without slaves. Since he was a fellow agriculturist rather than a capitalist in the eyes of his less wealthy neighbors, the sharp political dissensions which agitated the Tennessee Valley lost their sting in the southern part of the state.

Perhaps the best expanse of land in all this region lay in the vicinity of Montgomery County, and here there grew up what was probably an ideal planting community. The inhabitants are pictured as peace-loving, industrious, and economically independent. Instead of dealing with the local merchants, they car-

FIGURE 15: Cotton Crop of South Alabama

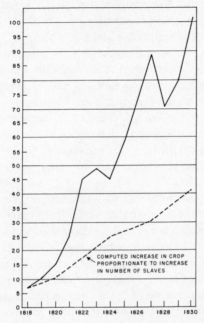

Hazard, *U.S. Commercial and Statistical Register* . . . , 6 vols.
(Philadelphia, 1840-42), III, 272

ried their cotton to Mobile and brought their supplies back up
the river.[46]

Even though indications show that the agricultural system
practiced in this region was more conservative than that in the
Tennessee Valley and there was less over-planting of cotton, yet
large quantities of pork and corn were imported along with
flour and whisky. Though some of this came down through the
country from Tennessee, the bulk of it came from Mobile, to
which point it had been shipped from the Ohio and Cumberland
River region by way of New Orleans. It was said in 1824 that
from 20,000 to 30,000 barrels of such supplies passed through
Mobile annually.[47]

The piney region of sandy clay which covers the southeastern corner of Alabama was considered relatively infertile, and here men without slaves or property set up a frontier community at the time when the rest of the state was being settled. Lands in the backwoods sections did not begin to be sold until about 1824, so that the immigrants could squat for years upon government property and then buy their farms at the minimum price after the speculative period was well over. Coming principally from Georgia, South Carolina, and Tennessee, the inhabitants of this region had the same general characteristics as those of the hilly region. The pasturage here made it possible for cattle to sustain themselves during the entire year, and large herds were kept by many of the settlers.[48]

Thus the agricultural life of Alabama may be divided into two predominant phases: that in which the planter, with a highly capitalized establishment, raised cotton with slave labor for the sake of profit; and that in which the farmer, with very little capital, sought an independent existence for his family. To the planter, rich lands and convenient water transportation were essential, while the price of cotton was of prime importance. To the farmer, transportation facilities were of little importance, and a large part of the state offered him isolated bits of good land which would have been of no value to the planter. The geographical segregation of these two classes of people was not complete, but there was little active competition between them. The best cotton lands were sold during the speculative period when the man without capital had little chance of successful competition; the backlands were sold during a later period when the actual settler could buy them at the minimum price with money which he had made from the ground. Though there was a tendency for the planter to displace the farmer who had settled in his immediate neighborhood, the lines which separated the planting districts from the farming districts were laid down when the government first opened the lands to settlers.[49]

CHAPTER EIGHT

Rivers and Roads

THERE IS NO WAY OF REALIZING MORE KEENLY the difference between past and present than to look upon the untroubled waters of a navigable river and recall that it once shaped the history of a section. Though the turbid stream of the Alabama now rarely floats a vessel, it is fitting that it gave its name to the state that it traverses. It was their separate waterway which gave the settlers along the Tombigbee interests which were disinct from those of settlers upon the lower Mississippi. It was down the streams that the early planters intended to float their cotton to market, and so they chose their lands near the rivers. (See figure 16.)

Mobile was a struggling community of 300 inhabitants, mostly Creoles, when it was taken over by the Americans in 1813. A few years later, when population began to spread along its tributary rivers, it began to grow and in 1819 numbered 800 inhabitants. In 1823 this number had increased to nearly 3,000.[1] Most of the higher class of Creoles had left when Spanish rule ended, and the new population was made up of Americans from every walk of life. Merchants came largely from the north, adventurers gathered from every quarter, and the mixture, according to some visitors at least, was not attractive.[2]

In place of the one wharf of Creole days, there were a dozen by 1823. Markets were built and brick structures began to replace wooden buildings. Because of obstruction in the harbor,

FIGURE 16: River map

large ships entered with difficulty. This fact made it necessary for the town to confine its shipping largely to coastwise traffic. Fruits from Cuba were to be found in the markets and a regular trade with New York was established at an early date, but most of the cotton destined for Europe had to be sent to New Orleans for shipment.[3]

The cotton region along the rivers gave birth to several towns between 1815 and 1818. St. Stephens already stood at the head of schooner navigation on the Tombigbee. It had been a flourishing little community when Mobile was still in the hands of Spain, but now the trade passed it by and went down to the larger town on the Bay. It still held a local trade, however, and some of its glory lingered. With its bank, its academy, its press, its land office, and its steamboat company, it maintained its place for a while; but its well-built houses were destined to sink into ruins which have now all but disappeared from view.[4]

Far above St. Stephens was Tuscaloosa, located at the head of boat navigation on the Black Warrior, and from here such overland trade as there was between the two sections of the state passed through Jones Valley to the Valley of the Tennessee.[5]

On the Alabama River, Claiborne grew up at the head of schooner navigation and. came to be the center of a cotton-planting community. The capital of the state was established at Cahawba, where the river of that name flows into the Alabama; and Selma was founded a few miles above. On a bluff not far from the head of navigation, two towns were built by land speculators in 1817 and 1818. One of these was founded by Andrew Dexter from Massachusetts, and was christened New Philadelphia; the other was founded by the Bibb Company and named East Alabama. In 1819 the two settlements were combined and incorporated as the town of Montgomery.[6]

From these places, the cotton passed down the rivers to Mobile. Flat-bottomed boats—crudely constructed affairs with pitched seams—could carry from fifty to a hundred bales and were broken up at the end of the journey.[7] Keel boats, though not used as frequently as flat-bottomed boats on the Alabama and Tombigbee, were employed where the requirements were more severe. They were frequently about fifty feet in length and were more durable and sea-worthy than the flat-bottomed type. But the greater expense of construction discouraged their use except where a return trip was to be made.

Nor were return trips very frequent. A boat which would float down from Montgomery to Mobile in about two weeks required a month or six weeks to be poled or warped back up the river; and the freight rate prevailing at that time was $5.00 a barrel.[8] Merchants generally preferred to bring their wares over the Federal Road from Georgia,[9] or down from the upper country. Whisky, pork, and flour were the most generally desired commodities in the cotton section. These articles, which could be obtained in East Tennessee and in western Virginia, were loaded on a keel boat near the place of production and floated down the Holston to the Tennessee River. By ascending a small tributary of the Tennessee, the Hiwassee, the boat could be navigated to within twelve miles of the headwaters of the Coosa. There was a portage across this stretch of land over which about 12,000 gallons of whisky were said to have been carried in 1821.[10] Boat houses were constructed at either end of it, and arrangements were made for hauling the boats in wagons from one stream to the other. This route was traversed at a very early period in Alabama history. Tennessee produce reached Montgomery by this course.

Transportation conditions in the Tennessee Valley were rendered peculiar by the obstruction in the channel of the river at Muscle Shoals. During the dry summer months the shoals could not be passed, but the river rose in the fall, and by February, boats could go over the rapids. The water began to go down again in the spring, so that only two or three months elapsed during which shipments could be made from above the shoals.[11] Warehouses were built at landing places on the river and here cotton was accumulated by merchants and shippers. As soon as the water rose, the bales were loaded on keel boats which were dispatched in fleets under the charge of experienced pilots who saw them safely past the shoals. The pilots would then return, and the boats would proceed to New Orleans under the direction of forwarding agents. The freight rate for cotton shipped in this manner was from $4.00 to $5.00 a bale.[12]

But difficult as it was to get cotton to market, it was still more difficult to bring back the needed supplies. There were several possible routes and all of them seem to have been used at times. Until 1816 the usual method was to ship goods from New York and Philadelphia to Charleston or Savannah; transport them to Augusta, and thence carry them by the Georgia Road through the Cherokee country to Ross's landing, opposite the spot where Chattanooga now stands on the Tennessee. From this point they were floated down to Ditto's Landing near Huntsville, or to other points along the river. In 1816 a merchant named Crump was the first to bring goods from Mobile to Huntsville by poling them up the river in a boat to Tuscaloosa, and from there hauling them in wagons. The road was found to be fairly good, and the overland trip required only eight days.[13] Supplies might also be brought through the Valley of Virginia by way of Knoxville; but the favorite route during the 'twenties seems to have been that down the Ohio to the Cumberland, up the Cumberland to Nashville, and across country from that place. Flour, pork, and whisky could be brought from Kentucky and the Northwest in this way, as could manufactures which went overland from Philadelphia to Pittsburgh and then down the Ohio.[14]

With the advent of the steamboat, conditions were radically changed. Goods could now be carried up stream as easily as they could be brought down, and the overland trade rapidly decreased. Central and southern Alabama became dependent upon Mobile for supplies while North Alabama began to obtain most of hers from New Orleans. The planter thus came in time to buy his goods at the same market in which he sold his cotton.

The first appearance of the steamboat on the rivers of Alabama cannot be fixed with absolute precision, but it seems clear that steam navigation on the Tombigbee was established in 1819. Morse's *Universal Geography* of that year states that steamers were then plying between Mobile and St. Stephens;[15] and Hamilton asserts in his *Colonial Mobile* that the first trip up to Demopolis was made in 1819 by either the *Tensa* or the *Mobile*.[16] There is a record of the launching of the *Tensa* on the Bay during this year, and the citizens of Mobile were a little later congratulated in the local press on another attempt to navigate the river.[17] During the same season the steamboat *Mobile*, which had been brought from Boston, was advertised to ascend to Tuscaloosa.[18]

It was not long before the *Harriett* and the *Cotton Plant* were brought to Mobile for service in the river trade, and in 1820 the *Tombeckbee* was launched at St. Stephens. This last boat was of seventy tons burden, had an eighty-five foot deck, and drew only fifteen inches of water when unloaded.[19] The others were about the same size, but little larger than the average keel boat then in use. But these four small craft were pioneers; they established steam communication on the waters of southern Alabama. In 1821 the *Harriett* ascended the Alabama to Montgomery; in 1824 the *Cotton Plant* made her way up the Tombigbee to the head of navigation at Cotton Gin Port, Mississippi;[20] and in 1828 the first trip was made up the Chattahoochee to the falls at Columbus, Georgia.[21]

It was during the fall and winter months only that the stage of the water was high enough to permit navigation of these rivers. Dread of yellow fever all but cleared Mobile of population during the summer; but in November the merchants began to return and collect their wares. The cotton trade commenced in this month and continued briskly until the following May or June; then it fell off suddenly and remained at a standstill until the waters rose in the fall.[22]

The number of boats on the rivers increased from year to year. In 1823 there were eleven,[23] and by 1826 the number had risen to eighteen.[24] All of these were vessels of light draft, the lightest being used in the Tuscaloosa trade. Cotton was piled high on the decks and passengers confined closely to the cabins, which were not commodious. Before reaching a town, a gun was fired from

the deck in order to warn inhabitants of the vessel's approach.
The banks of the rivers were generally steep and high, and cotton was loaded by sliding it down an inclined plane. The boats
frequently lay to in order to take on wood, and they always
stopped over night because of the many dangers which were to be
encountered in the tortuous streams. Striking a snag and sinking
was no infrequent occurrence.[25] Twice within the same season
the *Cotton Plant* succumbed to that fate, but each time she was
raised and sent on her way.

In the Tennessee Valley the transportation problem was peculiar. Huntsville, the largest town in the region, was built
around a great spring some ten miles from the river, and a considerable distance above the shoals. Florence and Tuscumbia
grew up where the Natchez Trace crossed the shoals. They had
some forwarding business in connection with shipping down the
Tennessee, but there was little return trade in the early years.

The first steamboat to reach Florence, as far as records show,
came in 1821.[26] From that time forward development was rapid.
It was only the next year that a small vessel, the *Rocket*, was
commissioned to run regularly between Florence and the mouth
of the river, depositing its cargo at Trinity to be forwarded up
the Ohio or down the Mississippi in larger vessels.[27] Regular
lines were later established to connect Tuscumbia with New
Orleans and the towns along the Ohio.[28]

Commercial conditions in the Tennessee Valley were changed
by these improvements in communication. The shippers above
the shoals continued to send their cotton down in keel boats, but
after the passage over the rapids, they were often towed to New
Orleans by the steamers, or their cargoes were transferred to the
larger vessels. Freight rates to New Orleans fell from more than
$1.00 a hundred-weight to 80 cents in 1822 and to 50 cents in
1828.[29]

Keel boats still came to Florence from the upper waters of the
Ohio, and merchants in the vicinity of Huntsville still brought
goods down from Nashville; but the steamboats which came up
to Florence brought large quantities of produce from New Or-

leans, and this came to be the main source of supply for the entire Valley region.

One further advance in transportation facilities was made when, in 1828, the little steamer *Atlas* ascended the shoals and began to ply the Tennessee between the rapids and the town of Knoxville.[30]

The introduction of steam navigation made more evident than ever the desirability of overcoming the obstruction at Muscle Shoals by means of a canal. The question was taken up by the legislature in 1823 and was under discussion for several years. Two successive companies were incorporated by the state for the construction of the desired canal, but the proposition did not prove sufficiently attractive to private investors and nothing was accomplished.[31]

Hope was aroused in 1824 by an act of Congress which appropriated money for the survey of an extensive system of internal improvements. John C. Calhoun, then Secretary of War, was called upon to submit a report on the subject, and the Muscle Shoals canal was among the works which he classed as of national importance.[32] A government survey was made and a report submitted.[33] But Congress was not acknowledged as having the right to appropriate funds for the construction of such works, and it seemed that the matter would be dropped. Yet there was no objection to the donation of land to states for the purpose of internal improvements. In 1828 Congress granted to Alabama 400,000 acres of relinquished lands in the Huntsville district, proceeds from the sale of which were to be applied to the construction of a steamboat canal around the shoals.[34]

While the people of the northern section of the state were interesting themselves in this project, those of South Alabama were working for a canal to connect the waters of the Tennessee with the Alabama River. Such a canal would enable the inhabitants of East Tennessee and western Virginia to ship their produce to Mobile, which was a much closer market than New Orleans. But the main consideration was that the people of South Alabama would be able to purchase their flour, whisky, and pork directly from East Tennessee instead of having to bring it around by New Orleans and Mobile.

This plan did not look unreasonable, for the route of the canal was to be the portage between the Hiwassee and the Coosa, which covered a distance of only twelve miles of moderately elevated land. The legislature, in order to enlist the support of both sections of the state, made a practice of dealing with both canal projects at the same time. A company was incorporated and empowered to co-operate with any company which Tennessee should establish for the construction of the Coosa-Hiwassee canal, the reason for this being that the site of the proposed work lay within the lands of the Cherokee Indians above the Tennessee line.[35]

Calhoun considered the Coosa-Hiwassee canal in his report of 1824, but classed it as being of less national importance than the canel suggested for Muscle Shoals. Though a government survey was made and a report presented,[36] the scheme for connecting the waters of the Alabama and Tennessee never recovered from this setback, while the Muscle Shoals project forged ahead.

During this period commerce was largely confined to the waterways, but most travelers were forced to use the primitive roads. They had to content themselves with log cabin accommodations as they passed through the forests, and the town inns were not attractive. It was a frequent occurrence for vehicles to be upset at some danger to life and limb, and consequently most journeys were made on horseback. The construction of a road consisted merely of cutting a passage through the woods, the stumps being left several inches above the ground. Bogs were traversed by causeways made of small logs placed close together across the road with dirt thrown on top. Bridges were not ordinarily built across the fordable streams, but ferries were established at river crossings.

Instead of going through the southern capitals, the mail from Washington to New Orleans went through the Valley of Virginia and by Huntsville until 1827. From Huntsville it was carried to Tuscumbia and thence followed the Natchez Trace.[37] As far as Huntsville, there was something that could be called a road, but the Natchez Trace was reported to be nothing more than a broad grass path.[38] The route was circuitous, and in 1816 Congress made an appropriation to enable Andrew Jackson to cut a direct road from Tennessee to New Orleans.[39] Troops were employed on this work, which was begun in 1817 and completed in 1820. It diverged from the old Trace at Muscle Shoals, and, passing Columbus, Mississippi, on the Tombigbee River, took a straight course to Madisonville, opposite New Orleans on Lake Ponchartrain.[40]

This Military Road, as it was called, was forty feet wide, had bridges over the smaller streams, and well-constructed causeways over the marshy places. But no provisions were made for keeping it in repair, and since the Trace passed through the settlements on the Mississippi while the Military Road lay through a region largely uninhabited, the latter was allowed to fall into disrepair. By 1824 the bridges had mostly been washed away and a growth of young trees was flourishing in the road itself. Though it was intended that the mail should have passed this way to New Orleans, it became necessary to cross over below Columbus and continue to take it along the old Trace route.[41]

The road to Huntsville was at first a mere branch of the main thoroughfare between Knoxville and Nashville, but it afforded a more direct route to New Orleans and was used for transporting mail after 1822. In 1820 Huntsville was made the terminus of the first stage line in Alabama. It connected with the main line between Knoxville and Nashville, and at first provided only weekly service.[42] This was increased in 1823 to two trips each way every week.[43] In 1825 an increase to three trips a week was made, and the line was extended to Tuscumbia.[44] Stages also connected Tuscumbia with Kentucky and Ohio by the route through Zanesville, Lexington, and Nashville.[45] But below Tuscumbia, the river did not permit continuous navigation and the Natchez Trace did not accommodate stages. Consequently, from Tuscumbia to New Orleans the mails were still carried in saddlebags.

The route through the southern capitals, instead of paralleling the streams as did the one through Huntsville, crossed them and hence was more subject to interruption from swollen waters. Though it lay through more populous communities than did the western route, the through mail between Washington and New Orleans was not carried along it until the latter part of 1827.[46] For this reason stage facilities on the road between Milledgeville, Montgomery, and Mobile developed later. The first stage route from Montgomery eastward was established in 1821. At first only one trip a week was made, but this was increased in 1823 to two trips weekly. Not until 1826 was there a regular line established between Montgomery and Milledgeville providing for three trips weekly.[47] It was during the next year that the through mail to New Orleans began to take this route. Mail was carried from Montgomery to Mobile in two-horse wagons, from Mobile to Pascagoula by sulkey, and from Pascagoula to New Orleans by steam packet.[48]

Though transportation actually developed only to this extent in early Alabama, a great deal of futile discussion was aroused by the Congressional Act of 1824 which provided for the survey of a system of internal improvements. Calhoun, in his report on the subject, stated that a highway from Washington to New Orleans would be best calculated to further the interests of the region through which it passed, and the survey of three separate routes was planned. The first of these was to cross the eastward-flowing rivers at their fall lines; the second was to lie between this and the Appalachian Mountains; and the third was to pass down the Great Valley beyond the mountains.[49] The surveys were accordingly made. The first two routes recommended were already followed by lines of travel. One lay through the southern capitals, passing on to Mobile; the second diverged from this in northern Virginia and passed through the piedmont towns of Petersburg, Salisbury, Greenville, and Athens, rejoining the other routes near the point at which it entered Alabama. But the third route differed from that already established. After passing through the Great Valley to Knoxville, instead of proceeding to Huntsville, it followed the valley of the Tennessee to where Chattanooga now stands, then, paralleling Lookout Mountain, passed into the valley of the Cahawba. From Centerville, at the falls of the Cahawba, it turned westward, leaving the state at Demopolis.[50]

This route followed the course of the rivers and valleys, and, theoretically, was perhaps the best. But it had the same disadvantage as Jackson's Military Road in that it did not follow an established route of travel. The Huntsville people proclaimed loudly that the route through their town should be surveyed, and they had their way.[51] The mail then took the Huntsville course to New Orleans, with the approval of the postmaster general. After the survey was made, no further action was ever taken. The Old South stood opposed to the policy of internal improvements, and shortly, with Jackson's aid, it was able to restrain the desires of those who would have the federal government construct a system of communication for the country.

Commercially distant as the two sections of Alabama were, there was necessarily some communication between them. The first route traveled from north to south seems to have been the portage between Muscle Shoals and the head of navigation on the Tombigbee at Cotton Gin Port. Pioneers floating down the Tennessee took this trail in order to reach the settlements in the neighborhood of St. Stephens.[52] Jackson, during the Creek War, cut a road from Huntsville southward through the country east of the Coosa River to the place where Fort Jackson was established at the confluence of the Coosa with the Tallapoosa.[53] By this route travelers were able to reach the Federal Road in the neighborhood of Montgomery.

Yet there was but one passage between North and South Alabama which came to be traveled with frequency, and that was the one which led from Huntsville through Jones Valley to Tuscaloosa at the head of navigation on the Black Warrior.[54] The road through the Valley was good, and much produce came down from Tennessee and reached central and southern Alabama by this route.[55]

CHAPTER NINE

The Commercial Situation

THE LACK OF A WELL DEVELOPED FINANCIAL SYS-
tem in the United States rendered commercial transactions much
more complicated in the 'twenties than similar business would
be today. Instead of a currency of uniform value resting upon the
credit of the government, there were only bank notes, the value
of which depended upon the credit of the issuing banks.

The first Bank of the United States had done much to stabilize
the condition of the currency, but this institution had gone out
of operation in 1811 and the end of the War of 1812 found the
country flooded with paper money which was no longer redeemed in specie by the banks which issued it. It was during this
period that settlers began to find their way into the Alabama
country in increasing numbers, and practically the only money
which permeated this frontier consisted of the depreciated notes
of the banks of Georgia.[1]

State banks were forced to resume specie payments when the
second Bank of the United States went into operation in 1817,
and the immigrants to Alabama were supplied with funds by the
numerous new banks which sprang up in Tennessee and Kentucky in 1818.[2] But the financial stress of 1819 caused these institutions to close their doors and leave their notes to circulate
at a depreciated value in the western country.

In 1816 the legislature of the Mississippi Territory had chartered the Merchants' and Planters' Bank of Huntsville, and in

1818 the Tombeckbee Bank of St. Stephens and the Bank of Mobile were chartered in the Alabama Territory. The two last-named institutions were not seriously affected by the events in Tennessee, for there were few commercial ties between South Alabama and that state; but the interests of the Huntsville region and specifically the Huntsville bank were necessarily affected by the affairs of the Tennessee banks.

The West was a debtor section; it owed for lands, for slaves, for goods. The East was creditor and had to be paid. But when the banks of Tennessee suspended specie payments, their notes were no longer available for remittance to the East. One way around the difficulty lay in purchasing Huntsville notes with the Tennessee notes, and drawing specie on the former, a procedure which put so great a drain on the specie reserve of the Huntsville bank that it felt itself forced to suspend payments in 1820.[3] Its notes continued to be used, but they fell below par and usually circulated at the same value as notes from Tennessee. Specie and the notes of specie-paying banks, now at a premium, ceased to pass from hand to hand, and North Alabama was left with a depreciated currency.[4]

The value of a bank note depended not only upon the solvency of the issuing institution, but upon the chance of presenting it for payment in specie. Thus the value of a note in a locality at some distance from the place of issue would depend upon the commercial relations between the two places. If the merchants who held the notes had no remittances to make to the place where they could be redeemed, they would have to bear the expense of sending them for redemption and bringing back the specie. The value of the notes would be diminished by the amount of this expense. If, for instance, it cost 5.0 percent to collect in this way, notes would be worth only 95 percent of their face value. But if the merchants had remittances to make, notes would be more convenient for that purpose than specie and they would command their full value. In fact, if the remittance to be made outran the supply of notes, the value of these might rise above their face value by the amount that it would cost to ship

FIGURE 17: Imports and exports at Mobile

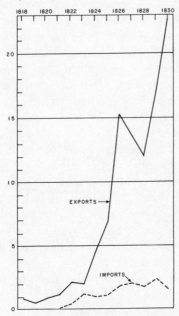

John MacGregor, *Commercial Statistics*, 5 vols.
(London, 1844-50), III, 289

specie in their stead. For instance, if it cost $3.00 to send $100 in specie, a $100 note would be worth $103 to a merchant who had remittances to make.

In Alabama, Georgia and South Carolina notes, which formed the bulk of currency in the southern part of the state, were worth about 4.0 percent less than specie in the Tennessee Valley because there was very little business between that section and the country directly to the south or east of it. The notes of New Orleans banks were usually on a par with these because the cotton sent down to the port was more than sufficient to cover all remittances for goods. But, on the other hand, the notes on Virginia banks and on the banks of Baltimore, Philadelphia, and New York were always nearly equal to specie because the Tennessee Valley imported its manufactured goods through the eastern cities and obtained its agricultural produce from the Ohio River region and from Tennessee. Eastern notes could be used to pay the East directly, or they could be employed with equal facility to pay the West, for the latter section was in debt to the former and anxious to have funds for remittance.[5]

So difficult was communication between the two sections of Alabama that the trade of the southern section was entirely distinct from that of the northern. Not only did the towns along the southern rivers send their cotton down to Mobile, but the central hilly region also forwarded its crops by way of Tuscaloosa and Montgomery. Some of the staple was shipped directly from Mobile to European ports, but the greater part went to eastern cities, principally New York.[6] An amount almost as great, consisting largely of the best grades, which could be passed off as the Louisiana product, was sent to New Orleans to pay for the corn, pork, flour, and whisky which came down from the Ohio River region and which were purchased by the merchants of Mobile to be sent up the Alabama and Tombigbee rivers to the interior of the state.[7]

In the trade between Mobile and the eastern cities, there was a balance in favor of Mobile, since more cotton was being shipped than was necessary to pay for the imports received in return. (See figure 17.) As a result, there was a balance due the southern merchants which had to be paid in cash. But in the trade with New Orleans the cotton shipped was not sufficient to pay for the produce that was imported, and the Mobile merchants had to use their cash to pay the difference.[8] In other words, the money which the planters of southern Alabama received for their cotton was spent largely in payment for corn, pork, flour, and whisky which were brought down the Ohio, Tennessee and Cumberland rivers to New Orleans, and shipped thence to Mobile.

The larger planters usually went down to Mobile once a year to transact their business with the merchants of the port; but the smaller producers had to do their business with country merchants who bought their goods in Mobile and transported them to the interior. These merchants did a local factorage business, which consisted of advancing supplies to farmers and taking their cotton in payment when the crop was made, a balance being struck once a year. The transactions between the larger planters and the merchants in the principal towns were perhaps frequently on this same basis.[9] This was the method whereby the cotton producer secured capital to finance his operations throughout the year. This capital was obtained in the first instance from local merchants who were in turn financed by eastern merchants for whom they purchased the staple. In this way the East furnished capital for the production of cotton.

During the early 'twenties, when the country was just being opened up, money was scarce in southern Alabama and many complaints were heard on the subject.[10] Yet the notes of the local banks, as well as those of South Carolina and Georgia, furnished a sound, though limited, currency.[11] So complete was the commercial separation between the two sections of the state, that each kept to its own medium of exchange with practically no interference from the other. After business conditions became more settled, the notes of South Carolina and Georgia banks ceased to pass at face value because of the lack of trade between Mobile and those states. A currency sufficient for practical purposes was furnished by local banks, the Bank of the United States, and the New Orleans banks.[12]

The specie foundation upon which all these notes rested was very slight, judged by modern standards. Both gold and silver were legal tender according to law, but according to the market prices of the metals, a gold dollar was worth more than a silver one. The result was that silver passed from hand to hand, while gold was withdrawn from circulation and a premium had to be paid to obtain it.

But even silver was scarce. There had been a profit made out of sending silver dollars to Latin American countries and exchanging them on equal terms for Spanish dollars, or pieces of eight *reales*, which were a little heavier. These foreign coins were brought back and melted down because the silver in them was worth a little more than a dollar according to our monetary standard. Hence there was left for circulation in this country only the Spanish dollars which were too light to afford a profit in the bullion market, and a certain amount of fractional Spanish coin.

This situation had caused Jefferson to suspend the coinage of silver dollars in 1806 and none had been produced since.[13] Spanish, Mexican, and other foreign coins made up our supply of specie, and it afforded a very light reserve against the notes which were issued by the banks, nor were there nearly enough of the smaller coins to serve the ordinary purposes of trade. A remedy was sought in the issue of "change tickets," which were merely bits of paper purporting to be worth twenty-five, fifty or seventy-five cents. They were signed by the issuer and were supposed to be redeemable for specie, but, since there was a demand for them, they were expected to remain afloat. This was a very profitable form of printing, and it was indulged in by business houses and municipal authorities.[14] The irregularity in the issuance of such tickets made this practice a great nuisance to the community. Forgeries were easy, and the country was flooded with the paper of various uncertain houses. These considerations finally induced the state to take the matter up; the issuance of change tickets by private firms was forbidden and the government undertook to furnish the people with a lawful supply.[15]

Such was the condition of the currency in Alabama, but the man who had cotton to sell was affected not only by local conditions, but by national and international trade relations as well. The crop of Alabama was sold largely through Mobile and New Orleans merchants, who in turn disposed of the bulk of it, directly or indirectly, in the British market. The American merchant collected his account by drawing a bill of exchange on the British purchaser and disposing of this to some other American merchant who was in need of funds to remit to England.

During the period following the War of 1812, America was importing more than she was exporting and the bills of exchange drawn by exporters were not sufficient to meet the demand of the importers who needed funds for remittance. The result was that some of the importers had to send gold to pay their debt, an operation which cost about 10 percent. It normally cost only about 5.0 percent to ship gold to England, but that country was on a gold basis and nothing but silver was circulating in this country. Consequently, the man who had a remittance to make in specie had to take silver at the current rate and purchase gold with it at about 5.0 percent advance. This premium on gold, added to the expense of shipment, accounts for the 10 percent which it cost to send specie to London. Now the man who could buy a bill of exchange on London to cover his debt was willing to pay—and the competition for such bills forced him to pay— a premium of about 10 percent over its face value.[16]

The Mobile merchants usually transacted their foreign business through New York firms, and received the proceeds of their foreign exchange in drafts on New York. Since, after the first few years of expansion, the cotton crop of South Alabama brought in more of these than could be used for remittances to New York, the balance had to be sent for collection in specie, and it cost about 3.0 percent to bring the specie from New York to Mobile. Hence New York paper passed at about 3.0 percent below its face value in the Alabama port, and the local merchant, not caring to stand the 3.0 percent loss, made a practice of remitting to the planter in New York funds, leaving the latter to pay the cost of converting them into current money.[17] Yet, as a total result, there was a gain of about 7.0 percent to the cotton producer because of the condition of trade balance between the cotton region and the East on the one hand, and between this country and England on the other.

It must not be understood from this discussion, however, that there was a trade balance in favor of Alabama as against the rest of the world and that specie was pouring in. While money was coming in from New York, it was all going out in other directions, and the state was accumulating no capital in cash. Like all newly-opened country, Alabama was in debt.[18] The settlers owed for their lands and slaves, and for consumable goods. What they made from their crops, they invested in their establishments and there was no capital for commercial enterprises. This was doubtless due largely to the fact that cotton planting was the only occupation which was sure to give social prestige. Merchandising was carried on to a large extent by men from the North, and it was not regarded with great esteem by the agricultural community. The merchant was likely to be looked upon by the planter as a grasping inferior, while the poor man was apt to consider him an economic enemy.

Speculation, land grabbing, and graft of all kinds were the necessary accomplishments of a rush into new country where all were scrambling for a place and where the strong could use their strength to great advantage against the weak. The man without capital was largely at the mercy of the one who had it, as is well illustrated by the situation in the sale of the public lands.

The planter who bought his land and settled down to the business of raising cotton was not looked on with disfavor by any segment of the population, for his profits did not come from his neighbors. But the man who used his capital in a commercial way made his profits largely out of the community, and he often made too much. Thus the poorer men frequently looked with suspicion upon those who did business with them, a suspicion nowhere more manifest than in banking.

CHAPTER TEN

The Bank Question

THE MONEY WHICH COTTON BROUGHT INTO ALA-
bama during the 'twenties went out largely through the land
offices and for slaves, and the state was left without commercial
capital. Funds were needed to finance the cotton crop; to promote agricultural expansion; and, especially, to furnish the basis
for a sufficient circulating medium. The first of these needs was
met by the New York cotton dealers, for they financed merchants in the South who bought the staple on their account;
agricultural expansion was provided for by the planter's rein-
vestment of his profits; but there seemed to be no means of
securing a sufficient circulating medium except by local banks,
and this expedient was resorted to.

The difficult problem was to obtain sufficient capital for investment in banking enterprises. As such institutions are conducted today, with solid value behind their paper dollars, they
do not add greatly to the capital of the community, being merely
organizations for its efficient use. If this had been the case in
1820, they would not have met the requirements of the Southwest. A multiplication of capital was expected of them—the crea-
tion of money where none existed before. Yet promising as the
prospects of these money-making machines were, men would
have invested their funds in lands rather than in banks had they
not expected to borrow more than they put in—so great was the
lure of cotton in the eyes of the planting community. This situa-

tion must be understood before the bank question can be made clear.

The charter of the Merchants' and Planters' Bank of Huntsville was granted by the legislature of the Mississippi Territory in 1816, while the Mobile and St. Stephens banks were granted theirs by the legislature of the Alabama Territory in 1818, yet the provisions of all three documents were very similar. The capital of each institution was limited to $500,000, a minority of which was reserved to the territorial government in each case; no interest over 6.0 percent might be charged; and the issue of notes was not to exceed three times the amount of capital actually paid in.[1] This last provision indicates that the authorities were more solicitous for a currency than they were for financial safety. They evidently expected the banks to be money-manufacturing institutions, and their hopes were not disappointed.

In September, 1818, the Tombeckbee Bank of St. Stephens went into operation with only $7,700 of its stock subscribed. Israel Pickens, a lawyer of St. Stephens and register of the land office there, was elected president, and George S. Gaines, long-time factor for the Choctaw Indians, was chosen secretary.[2] In January, 1820, Pickens wrote to the Secretary of the Treasury that the Mobile bank had but a nominal existence. He stated that the institution, which had been chartered in 1818, had had $70,000 subscribed to its capital, and that one-eighth of this, or about $8,000 had been paid in specie. An agent was sent North with a part of this sum to secure the materials for putting the bank in operation, but while he was gone, the bank's balance was lost by robbery. Now the agents of the Mobile institution were supposed to be drawing upon the Tombeckbee Bank for specie with which to put their corporation on its feet.[3]

Meantime the Huntsville bank, being an older institution, was doing business in a larger way. In August, 1819, it had a capital of $164,000 and had discounted to the extent of $408,000.[4] The Secretary of the Treasury wrote to LeRoy Pope, president of the Huntsville bank,[5] as well as to the president of the Tombeckbee Bank,[6] and expostulated on the reckless way in which their affairs were being conducted, but no practical reform was effected. Demand for accommodation was great, capital was limited, and the temptation to profit was too strong to be withstood.

The first evident result of this situation was the suspension of specie payments by the Huntsville bank in 1820. The suspension of specie payments by the Tennessee banks in 1819 had been followed by a drain of specie from the Huntsville bank, a drain too heavy for an institution whose circulation far exceeded its specie reserve.[7] It was believed, however, that the bank was sound, and its notes continued to circulate on a par with those of the Tennessee banks. The two together made up the currency of northern Alabama.

Because of the lack of commercial relations between the two sections of the state, this financial trouble did not affect the south, where the two local banks continued to pay specie and where most of the circulation consisted of notes of the solvent banks of Georgia. The equilibrium of Alabama would hardly have been disturbed had not the situation developed a political as well as a commercial phase. As long as the Huntsville bank paid specie on its notes, they were, of course, received by the state in payment of taxes. But when the bank suspended payments, the legislature refused to debar its notes from acceptance.[8] The result of this was that all who could procure the depreciated notes turned them in to the treasury instead of sound funds, and the entire community suffered by the situation. In addition, the legislature, during the same session, emitted an issue of treasury notes which were made payable in Huntsville currency. The natural result was that they at once fell to a par with the Huntsville notes, and the state lost the difference.

Though the legislature could hardly have misunderstood the inevitable result of the course which it took in this matter, the governor defended its action by arguing that the people of northern Alabama could not secure other funds than the notes of the Huntsville bank, and that it would be unjust to refuse to let them pay their taxes with this money.[9] This governor was not the William Wyatt Bibb who had presided over the Territory

of Alabama and had been elected to the chief office under the
new state government. He had died in 1820 from the effects of
a fall from his horse, and was succeeded by his brother, Thomas
Bibb, president of the state Senate.[10] It is interesting to note in
this connection that Thomas Bibb was a director of the Huntsville bank in 1823.[11]

This confusion in financial affairs brought out more strongly
than ever the desire for a state bank. The three private banks in
operation had been chartered under territorial governments and
there was no intention of chartering any new ones under the
state. The constitution provided for a bank of the commonwealth, and efforts were soon on foot to found such an institution.

The first step in this direction was taken by the legislature in
1820. Provision was made for a state bank with a capital of
$2,000,000. Half of the stock was to be reserved to the state and
the government was to choose the president and six of the twelve
directors, thus controlling the institution.[12] Books were opened
for public subscription, but no capital was found for investment
in such a bank, and the scheme fell through.[13]

But the idea was not abandoned. In 1821 Israel Pickens succeeded Thomas Bibb as governor. Pickens came to Alabama from
North Carolina in 1817, having served his native state in Congress since 1811. He took up residence at St. Stephens and became president of the Tombeckbee Bank. Before Bibb retired
from office, commissioners had been appointed by the legislature
to negotiate with the private banks and to discover on what
terms they would be willing to become branches of a state bank.[14]
The constitution had provided that such an arrangement might
be made and, since other capital did not seem to be obtainable,
the idea of founding a state institution through the instrumental-
ity of those already existing appealed to many. A bill for carrying
this plan into effect was passed by the legislature, but was vetoed
by Governor Pickens at the inception of his term of office.[15] If
allowed to become law, this measure would have committed the
credit of the state into the hands of a few bankers without any

careful scrutiny of their affairs. Considering the way in which
the private banks of Alabama had been conducted, such a move
would have been dangerous, to say the least. There were many
who praised Pickens for stepping in to prevent it and there were
many who criticized him for his action.

The political division in Alabama had previously been due to
the rivalry between the north and the south of the state, or to the
antagonism which grew up against those Georgia men who,
through the friendship of William H. Crawford, enjoyed a practical monopoly of federal patronage. Now the bank question was
injected into the midst of the situation.

Though Pickens was not a Georgia man, his appointment as
register of the land office at St. Stephens would indicate that he
was not at odds with the Georgia faction. It is significant that
in 1819 he wrote a letter endorsing Dr. Henry Chambers, who
was running against Colonel John Crowell for a seat in the lower
House of Congress.[16] Dr. Chambers was from the Tennessee
Valley and represented the Georgia faction, while Crowell was
from the southern part of the state and not a Georgia man. In
1821 it was Chambers who opposed Pickens for the governorship, but he was a weak candidate and carried only a few of the
counties in his own section.[17]

No political issues seem to have been brought forward in this
campaign. The question of the currency and the state bank was
before the people and had been discussed at random, but no
definite line of action had been proposed. Pickens' attitude on
the subject does not appear to have been canvassed, but he no
sooner took his stand than a general agitation began.

The Huntsville bank had profited, or was thought to have
profited, at the expense of the people of the state, and the capital
of this institution was largely in the hands of men from Georgia.
The feeling against the bank was added to the feeling against the
Crawford faction, and those who shared these sentiments rose
up to proclaim Pickens the man who had saved his state from
the hands of the spoilers.[18]

The veto of the charter was followed by an attack on the

Huntsville bank. Its notes were debarred from acceptance in payment of debts to the state,[19] and this, together with the failure of the prospect that the institution would become a branch of the state bank, led to a rapid decline in their value. In all this, the newspapers of the state, which were edited largely by Adams men, supported the governor's action, the *Alabama Republican* of Huntsville being a notable exception.

But when it came to the constructive side of Pickens' program, there was a great difference of opinion. Private capital had failed to come to the support of a state managed bank in 1820, and the existing banks were not to be trusted with the destinies of a public institution. There was but one other possible chance, and the governor set his face in that direction: the state was to furnish its own capital and direct its own bank for the benefit of the people. For procuring the necessary funds, the state had but one recourse: the lands which had been granted to it by the national government. It was proposed that the proceeds from the sale of these lands be invested in the bank and the 6.0 percent interest be paid on the funds and devoted to the purpose for which the original grants had been made. The management of the institution was to be in the hands of a president and board of directors chosen by the legislature.[20]

The bearing of such a proposition in a state where the majority of the people were hard-pressed for money can easily be understood. Those who had some capital and a fairly intelligent interest in economic affairs would oppose it. Those who had no capital, wanted cheap money, and knew little of business methods, would favor it with all the ardor of frontier democracy. In other words, here was the material for a political cleavage along economic lines, but the governor who gave the popular party its rallying-ground was not a Jackson man.

Discussion of the question went on with unabated earnestness, but without practical results, during the whole of Pickens' first term in office. The *Alabama Republican* of Huntsville showed an unmistakable leaning toward the private banks, while the Mobile papers contended for a commercial rather than a democratic in-

stitution. It was argued with reason that unless the bank was
located at the center of trade, its notes would not circulate at
par at any distance from the place where they were issued and
could be redeemed.[21] It was also questioned whether a bank
would be efficiently administered under the auspices of the legislature. But the striking feature in the discussion was the appearance of a new paper in Huntsville called the *Democrat* and edited
by a man from Kentucky. In the fall of 1823 this publication
suddenly came forward and announced itself the champion of
"the people."[22] The people had been without a leader, it said, and
had suffered many things at the hands of the aristocrats. The
president of the Huntsville bank was accused of several kinds of
rascality, and the administration of the corporation was condemned as a robbery of the poor. It was alleged that cotton had
been shipped to New York, sold there for sound money and the
proceeds brought back to Huntsville and exchanged by the bank
for its own notes at a discount.[23] This process was known as
"shaving," and the term "shavers" was applied in opprobrium to
those connected with the bank. Color is lent to charges of this
kind by the fact that LeRoy Pope, president of the bank, who
was also pension agent, paid pensioners in the depreciated notes
of his institution, and was for this reason dismissed from his
office by the Treasury Department.[24]

Pickens was again candidate for the governorship in 1823. The
bank question was made a leading issue of the campaign,[25] and
his second election was followed shortly by the incorporation of
the Bank of the State of Alabama. The capital was to be derived
from the sale of lands donated to the state for the founding of a
university, from the 1,640 acres donated for a seat of government,
from the 3.0 percent which was taken out of the sale of federal
lands for the purpose of constructing roads within the state, and
from several minor sources. The amount of university money
which could be invested in this manner was limited to $100,000,
and $100,000 additional was to be borrowed on the credit of the
state. It was provided that 6.0 percent was to be paid on all
funds, and the interest on the university fund, the "three per

cent" fund, and other special funds, was to be devoted to the objects for which the original donations had been made. The bank was to be located at the seat of government, the president and directors were to be chosen by the legislature, and all discounts were to be apportioned among the several counties according to their representation in the legislature.[26] In the Senate, the vote on this measure was thirteen to six, with those who were in the negative representing the more commercial communities.[27]

In July, 1824, the bank was organized with a capital slightly in excess of $200,000, half of which was derived from the resources of the state, and the other half borrowed.[28] Its discounts soon exceeded its capital, and its notes began to constitute an appreciable part of the local circulation.

This addition to available money came at an opportune time, for several of the older issues of notes were shortly withdrawn from general use. The war against the Huntsville bank was carried on until 1825, when, because of its failure to redeem a pledge to resume specie payments, its charter was annulled.[29] Though all its notes were not withdrawn, they ceased to form any appreciable part of the circulating medium of the Tennessee Valley.

The Tennessee notes, which made up the greater part of the currency of the Valley, circulated in abundance as long as they were not redeemable, since eastern merchants who collected debts in Tennessee funds found it profitable to purchase cotton with them rather than to take them into a part of the country where they were at a great discount.[30] But in 1826, the Tennessee banks resumed specie payments and their notes ceased to circulate extensively in Alabama.[31] Thus the Huntsville region was left almost destitute of a currency, and "change tickets" appeared in great numbers despite the fact that their issuance was illegal.[32] A planter who sold his cotton in New Orleans and received a draft on New York in payment could realize cash on his paper by exchanging it in Nashville for "post notes" issued by the firm of Yeatman and Woods. These notes were made payable in Philadelphia several months after date, which arrangement put them at a discount and kept them in circulation so that they came to make up a large part of the currency in northern Alabama.[33]

In the meantime the southern part of the state was having its troubles. In 1826 the United States Bank established a branch at Mobile in spite of the protests of those who believed that it would be a menace to the Bank of Alabama.[34] The branch bank refused to receive the notes of local banks, but made an exception in the case of the Mobile bank provided that it would redeem its obligations at frequent intervals. In turn, the Mobile bank, in order to protect itself, refused to receive the notes of the St. Stephens bank and of the state bank unless they would redeem them at frequent intervals in Mobile. This was necessary because there was a flow of currency from the interior toward Mobile, but no counterflow to balance the situation. The state bank made terms, but the St. Stephens bank refused to do so and seems to have damaged its credit by the stand it took. At any rate, it closed its doors in 1827 and its notes ceased to pass as currency.[35]

By 1828 the capital of the state bank had increased to $409,000, and arrangements were made for borrowing another $100,000.[36] In addition to this, permission had been obtained from Congress to sell the sixteenth section in each township which had been donated for the establishment of public schools, and provision was made by the legislature for investing the proceeds in the bank.[37] The discounts of the institution were now more than $600,000; its notes in circulation amounted to $395,000, and its cash funds to $294,000.[38] Here was an establishment of portentous possibilities.

CHAPTER ELEVEN

Politics and the Election of 1824

With the influence of Georgia on the early politics of Alabama as strong as it was, unusual consequences were bound to arise. The fraudulent Yazoo land speculation had split Georgia into two factions; those who attacked and annulled the sales were led by General James Jackson, while the defenders adhered to General Elijah Clarke. In time the leadership of the Jackson party passed into the hands of William H. Crawford, while the opposition was maintained by John Clarke, son of the General.[1]

Between these factions there were no standing political differences, but the rivalry between the leaders on each side was backed by certain economic and sectional differences between their respective followings. There had been two centers of settlement in Georgia: one along the tidewater region where sea-island cotton formed the basis for a planting aristocracy, and the other in the piedmont region where the Savannah River cut through the red hills and afforded transportation facilities for planters of upland cotton. The older settlements were those of the tidewater region, but after the Revolution, while upland cotton was coming into its own, emigrants had come from Virginia and North Carolina and established themselves in the piedmont section. Elbert County came to be a center of Virginia influence, while Wilkes County, just to the north, became a center of North Carolina influence. A marked rivalry grew up between the two groups of settlers, each tending toward exclusiveness.

James Jackson, and later, George M. Troup, stood for the tidewater aristocracy, while Clarke represented the plain men of the frontier sections of the state. Crawford was a Virginian of the piedmont section, and his co-operation with Jackson brought about an alliance of the two groups which they represented. The North Carolinians were thus thrown into the arms of the Clarke party.

The majority of the leading men of the state were of the Crawford faction and for a long time they succeeded in maintaining political control. When the new lands in Alabama were opened up, however, the exodus of cotton planters was a severe blow to the party. A substantial number of wealthy Georgians, including LeRoy Pope and his son-in-law, John W. Walker, had gone from Elbert County and established Huntsville in 1809 and 1810. But it was in 1817 and 1818 that a great body of them bought land at the government sales at Milledgeville and moved out into the basin of the Alabama River to become the backbone of the planter class in that section.

It was during this time that Georgia's two senators, Charles Tait and William W. Bibb, voted for a bill to increase the salaries of members of their body. A storm of protest ensued which resulted in their withdrawal from Congress, and was instrumental in causing them to move to Alabama. Bibb at once became governor of the new Territory, but Tait remained in the Senate until the end of his term. Then, statehood having been obtained for Alabama, he reaped his reward for senatorial service by being made a district judge of the new commonwealth. These men were accompanied to Alabama by other strong supporters of Crawford, among whom was Bolling Hall, who had sat in the House of Representatives for his native state and who now took up residence in Autauga County across the river from Montgomery.

Governor Bibb was popular in Alabama, and Walker seems to have won his way to the Senate through sheer worth. Tait also had senatorial aspirations, but yielded to William R. King when jealousy of the Georgia group made it clear that it was dangerous to push too far. William H. Crawford, as Secretary of the Treasury, was not so cautious, however, in dispensing federal patronage in the state. He controlled practically all appointments and his friends were invariably put into office except when it became expedient to conciliate an opponent. Bait was held out to King in the hope of diverting him from his race for the Senate, but he refused to be diverted.[2] William Crawford, who succeeded Pickens as president of the Tombeckbee Bank, was district attorney and, at the same time, receiver for the St. Stephens land office. If the receiver had been irregular in his accounts, the attorney would hardly have been eager to prosecute the case![3]

This condition naturally aroused the anger of those who did not have a finger in the pie, and complaints of partisanship and inefficiency went up on all sides. It was not a struggle which would greatly concern the majority of the people, who were absorbed in other things, but it concerned the politicians and they, in turn, had some power to arouse the people.

This power seems to have been more limited than would be expected. There were no parties nor even any standing issues. The people, busy with their clearings and their crops, appear to have elected their more ambitious neighbors to represent them in the legislature, thus relieving themselves of burdensome political questions except those matters of immediate economic concern. No serious attempt was made to arouse them until Pickens seized upon the bank question and made an issue of it.

The relationship between the champion of the state bank and the Crawford men is not easy to trace. It is stated that Pickens, then a congressman from North Carolina, supported Crawford when he stood for the presidency against Monroe in 1816. But when Crawford refused to appoint him register of the land office at Cahawba, a position which had been promised him by Alexander J. Dallas, Secretary of the Treasury, Pickens turned against the Georgia men and threatened to become head of an opposition.[4] It was probably Tait who secured for Pickens the

FIGURE 18: Election of U.S. Senator, 1822

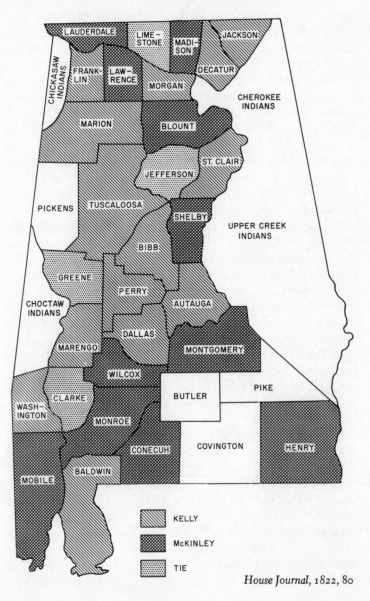

appointment as register of the land office at St. Stephens,[5] and this seems to have prevented hostilities until the gubernatorial campaign of 1821, when Pickens denied all connection with the Crawford party.[6]

Since Crawford stood for the aristocratic group in Georgia and the majority of his followers who came to Alabama were planters of some means, the connection of a few of them with the unfortunate Huntsville bank made it possible for their enemies to call them "opressors [sic] of the poor," and the fight for the state bank was made a fight against the Georgia faction. The challenge was accepted, and the Crawford men led the defense of the private banks, while their opponents combined against them to establish the "people's bank."[7]

It is an interesting alignment of factions that was brought about by this situation. Farmers on a small scale had come into Alabama primarily from Tennessee, Georgia, and South Carolina; but whatever their origin, they were preponderantly Andrew Jackson men. Among the planters there was no such unanimity. Those from Georgia were most numerous along the upper Alabama River, and they were the principal supporters of Crawford when he was candidate for President in 1824. Those from the Carolinas and Virginia predominated in the Tombigbee basin as far up as Tuscaloosa, and John Quincy Adams was strongest in this section. In the Tennessee Valley, the Georgia planters mingled with the planters from Virginia and the Carolinas and produced a variety of political sentiments, the Georgia influence being strong in Madison County but dwindling away toward the west. On the bank question, the Adams planters were allied with the Jackson farmers to defeat the Crawford men.[8]

The election of Pickens to the governorship was the beginning of hard times for the Georgia faction. They had at first made Alabama their own, and the new state was glad to have their powerful influence in Washington, though their monopoly of the federal patronage created enemies among the politicians from other states. In the untimely death of Governor Bibb, they lost a strong leader. This misfortune was followed in 1822 by

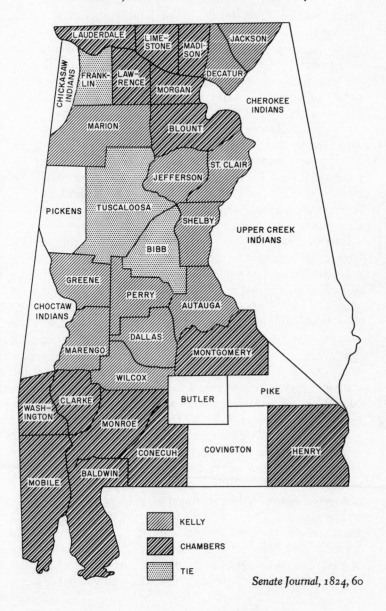

FIGURE 19: Election of U.S. Senator, 1824

KELLY

CHAMBERS

TIE

Senate Journal, 1824, 60

the resignation from the Senate of John W. Walker, whose death occurred in 1823. These two men had won much respect in the community, and there were no others of equal caliber to take their places. In the contest to fill the vacant seat in the Senate, the Crawford men supported John McKinley, while their opponents, the "friends of the people," backed William Kelly. The latter won the contest by a narrow majority, (see figure 18), and when the unexpired term was completed, he stood for re-election. This time he was defeated by Dr. Henry Chambers (see figure 19), whose victory restored the balance, for Alabama's second senator, William R. King, was from North Carolina and, like Pickens, no friend of the Georgia faction. (See figure 20.) King retained his seat continuously in the Senate for twenty-five years after Alabama became a state.[9]

But the Crawford men, while able to maintain political balance in the legislature, were not nearly so strong when elections went straight to the people. None of the early congressmen was of their number, nor were they able to elect a governor after 1819. It is indeed surprising to consider how small was the group of men who all but dominated the legislature of the state. The planters were few compared to the total number of settlers, nor did the Georgians constitute a majority of the planters, yet they made up the predominant class in an important section of the state and found their way into politics in relatively large numbers. This was possible because of their prominence as office-holders, because there were no organized parties, and because there was no standing antagonism between the planter and the farmer. There were politicians who wanted to encourage the people to recognize their rights, and in the matter of the bank they succeeded in their aim. But ordinarily the people did not feel a great need of instruction. In the absence of parties, politics was largely personal. Only men of some station thought of running for office, and the average voter selected his favorite candidate without questioning what he stood for. While a study of the popular elections shows very clearly that the people knew what they wanted when a matter of political interest was put squarely

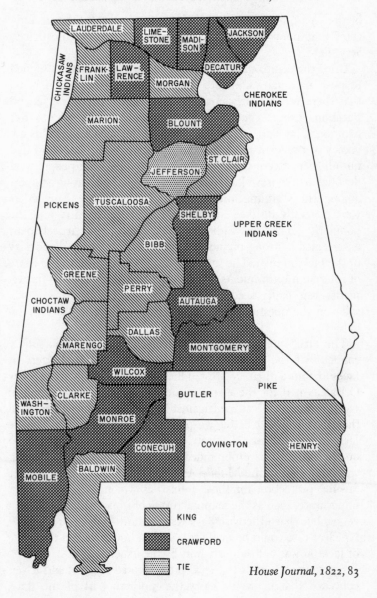

FIGURE 20: Election of U.S. Senator, 1822

House Journal, 1822, 83

before them, a comparison of the votes of the legislature indicates that popular control was, under ordinary circumstances, very slight.

Until the campaign of 1824 approached, local matters tended to push national issues into the background, the reason being that there was a nearly unanimous agreement upon all federal questions except the one of who should be President after Monroe. Clay had a few strong friends in Alabama, but his advocacy of the tariff rendered him unpopular; and Crawford had no followers except the Georgia planters. The plain people were devoted to Andrew Jackson, while Adams had strong support among the Carolina and Virginia planters. New Englanders were generally disliked in this section of the country and the popularity of Adams indicates that the conservative element entertained a strong prejudice against the aggressive democracy of the Jackson men. The support which Adams gave to the cause of internal improvements was an asset in a state where improvements were badly needed, and his friends claimed that he was safer on the question of the tariff than any of the other candidates.[10]

The tariff question was the disturbing one. Alabama solidly condemned the system of protection, and the supporters of Jackson found their greatest difficulty here. The hero of New Orleans voted for the increased duties that were established in 1824, a stand that was used against him by his enemies, nor could they have found a better weapon. It became necessary for the Jackson men to bestir themselves in the matter. A direct question on the subject was propounded to the General and his answer was published in the *Mobile Advertiser*. He said clearly that he favored protection for those industries which were of military importance, such as the manufacturing of iron and cheap woolen goods, but that otherwise he favored a tariff only for revenue.[11] No clear case could be made for Adams, however, and the cause of Jackson was not seriously hurt by the issue.

A strong section of the local press favored Adams, and it was conceded that he would carry the southern part of the state,

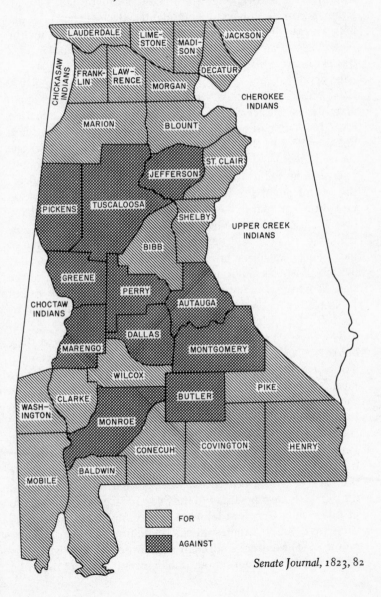

FIGURE 21: Senate vote on motion proposing Jackson for the presidency

FOR

AGAINST

Senate Journal, 1823, 82

while Jackson was expected to carry the northern half.[12] An attempt was made to have the presidential electors chosen by district with the hope that two of the five could be carried for the New England candidate,[13] but the plan was defeated and in 1823 the legislature declared that Jackson was the choice of the state.[14] (See figures 21 and 22.) So great was the General's popularity that even his enemies had to speak respectfully of him. Those members of the legislature who voted against the nomination took the trouble to explain that they did so, not because of hostility, but because they did not consider the question a proper one for legislative action.[15] Governor Pickens used the same grounds to explain his failure to sign the nominating resolution.[16] Indeed, the loss of popularity which one suffered by opposing Jackson brought many men to a new way of thinking. Dr. Henry Chambers was backed by the Georgia group when he ran for the governorship in 1821 and 1823,[17] but he became a supporter of Jackson and was made presidential elector on the popular ticket in 1824. Nicholas Davis, who for five years was president of the state Senate, was an opponent of the state bank and no friend of Jackson's,[18] conceded to the plan calling for his nomination by the legislature in 1823.

There was no regularly established political machinery in 1824, but co-operation was necessary in order to win a spirited contest. This was accomplished in an informal but effective way. Public meetings of the friends of several candidates were announced in the newspapers and held in the leading towns. Those attending the meetings proposed electoral tickets and chose committees of correspondence. At one such gathering held at the courthouse in Perry County on May 8, 1824, it was proposed that representatives be chosen by friends of Jackson in the various parts of the state and sent to a convention which would meet at Cahawba during the following session of the Supreme Court.[19] The friends of Adams and Crawford followed this example, and accordingly there were three conventions held in due time at the seat of government. These were informally constituted bodies, consisting of representatives from various public meetings and of men who

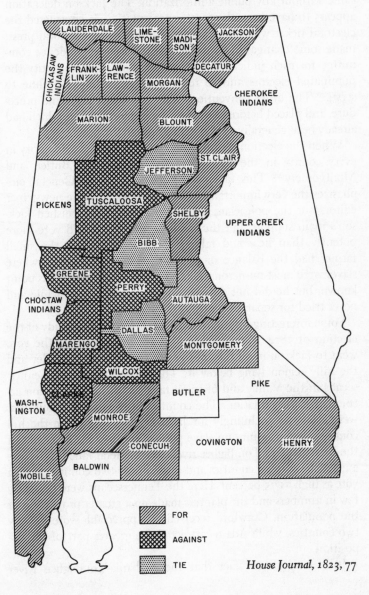

FIGURE 22: House vote on motion proposing
Jackson for the presidency

FOR

AGAINST

TIE

House Journal, 1823, 77

came without any public authorization. The Jackson delegation appears to have been the most representative. It considered the electoral ticket which had been promulgated by the local press, made some changes in it, and appointed a correspondence committee for each judicial circuit, authorizing them to notify the nominated electors and to replace any who might decline to serve.[20] The other conventions followed much the same procedure, and placed before the voters the electoral tickets which had already been generally agreed upon through the press.[21]

When the election returns came in, Jackson had a majority in every county in the state except three—Greene, Butler, and Montgomery.[22] This unexpected strength of the General emphasizes the very important point that it was not the newspaper editor, nor the politician, nor the planter who furnished Jackson's main support, but the small farmer who could vote more potently than he could talk. It became clear that the small farmer had the balance of power even in the counties where slaves were most numerous. He spoke clearly and made his point known, but he did not differ from the planter on principle and never tried for separate control.

Some interesting information is obtainable from a study of the election of 1824. (See figure 23.) Over 75 percent of the vote went to Jackson in all the counties of the Tennessee Valley and the hilly region lying below it. The predominance of Tennesseeans in the Valley and of small farmers in the hilly region accounts for this situation. The counties in the extreme southeast were also overwhelmingly for Jackson, and these, like the hill counties, had a minimum slave population. But in the basins of the Alabama and Tombigbee rivers, the General failed to receive a majority in three counties and carried only two counties with a vote as high as 75 percent. Here the Tennesseeans were relatively few in numbers and the planters made up a greater proportion of the population. Crawford received an appreciable vote in only two counties, while Adams attracted the greater part of the opposition.

It is a significant fact that the Alabama-Tombigbee River

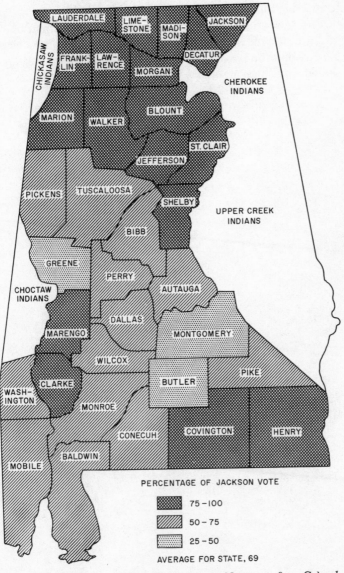

FIGURE 23: Presidential election of 1824

LAUDERDALE
LIME-STONE
MADISON
JACKSON
CHICKASAW INDIANS
FRANK-LIN
LAW-RENCE
DECATUR
MORGAN
CHEROKEE INDIANS
MARION
WALKER
BLOUNT
ST. CLAIR
JEFFERSON
PICKENS
TUSCALOOSA
SHELBY
UPPER CREEK INDIANS
BIBB
GREENE
PERRY
AUTAUGA
CHOCTAW INDIANS
DALLAS
MARENGO
MONTGOMERY
WILCOX
CLARKE
BUTLER
PIKE
WASH-INGTON
MONROE
CONECUH
COVINGTON
HENRY
MOBILE
BALDWIN

PERCENTAGE OF JACKSON VOTE

75 –100

50 – 75

25 – 50

AVERAGE FOR STATE, 69

Huntsville *Democrat*, Nov. 22, 1824. *Cahawba Press*, Nov. 22, 1824, *et seq.*

basin, which later became the stronghold of Whigism, was carried for Jackson in 1824, yet with a smaller margin than he obtained in the other sections of the state. There was the nucleus here among the planters for a strong fight when circumstances should furnish an argument which could attract allies.

CHAPTER TWELVE

Politics and Federal Relations, 1824-1828

AFTER THE ELECTION OF 1824, THERE WAS A
distinct change in the political situation in Alabama. No sooner
was Jackson defeated than his friends announced their determination to "fight the battle o'er again,"[1] and their opponents
recognized the futility of a further struggle against the General.
The administration was able to hold a few scattered supporters,
but even the *Southern Advocate* of Huntsville, which had been
an ardent friend of Adams before the election, now went over to
the cause of Jackson, though this change was clearly one of letter
rather than of spirit. Among the Crawford men the defection
was even more general. Their hero was no longer in the race, and
it was left for them to make the best terms they could for themselves. The new editor of the Huntsville *Democrat*, the acknowledged champion of "the People" in the state, admitted that he
had supported Crawford in 1824,[2] but former allegiance was not
held against any man in those days unless there was some special reason for doing so. When resolutions proposing Jackson for
the presidency were passed by the legislature in 1827 (see figure
24), their proponent was no other than Dixon H. Lewis, nephew
of Bolling Hall, and closely connected with all the supporters of
Crawford who had led the Georgia faction in Alabama. Adams
had to be beaten and only Jackson could beat him.

FIGURE 24: Vote on Lewis report proposing
Jackson for the presidency

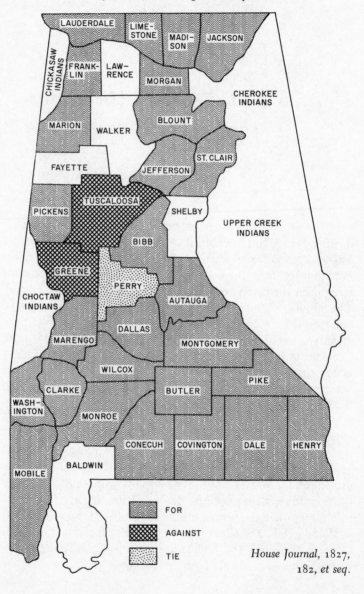

FOR

AGAINST

TIE

House Journal, 1827,
182, et seq.

Yet beneath this general accord regarding Jackson, there were political divisions on local questions which were more indicative of the true state of the public mind. In 1825 the term of Israel Pickens expired and John Murphy was elected to the governorship without opposition. Murphy, like Pickens, was from North Carolina, and a supporter of the state bank. His unopposed election indicates the complete triumph of the popular cause and is a tribute to the political sagacity of the retiring governor.

The first important question to come up was the location of the capital. The constitution had provided that, during the session of 1825, the legislature might remove the seat of government from Cahawba, but if no removal was made at that time, the original seat would be permanent. The subject was taken up with alacrity and several new locations were proposed. The fight developed mainly between Cahawba, favored by the southern and southeastern portions of the state, and Tuscaloosa, the choice of the northern and northwestern sections. Cahawba was accessible to the entire Alabama River region, while Tuscaloosa was more convenient to the Tennessee Valley and Tombigbee regions. In the final struggle, the Tennessee, Tombigbee, and Warrior valleys were able to outvote the Alabama River region, and the capital moved to Tuscaloosa.[3] (See figure 25.) Cahawba had proved to be an unhealthy location, but it was argued that Tuscaloosa was too near the Mississippi line, and there was little prospect that the capital could remain there after the Indian lands east of the Coosa River were opened up.

Such a question was not good for party purposes, but another issue came up at this time which was used for all it was worth by the office seekers.

In 1818 the legislature of the Alabama Territory had passed an act which abolished all limitations on the amount of interest which might be charged on loans. John W. Walker then wrote to Tait saying that he was largely responsible for the measure, and asked his friend what he thought of it.[4] This apparent self-aggrandizement on the part of the lawmakers aroused such strong opposition at the time that it was repealed the next year

FIGURE 25: Vote on bill fixing state capital at Tuscaloosa

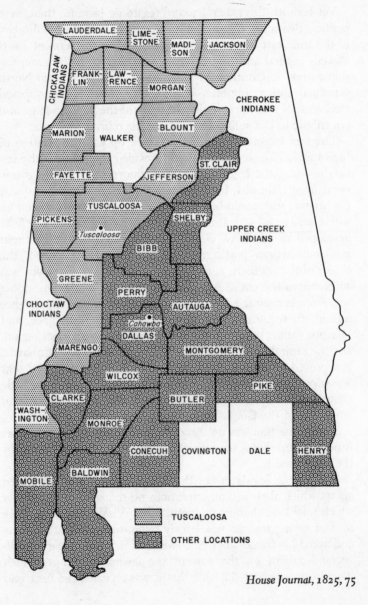

without struggle. In the meantime numerous contracts had been made under its provisions and the interest called for ranged from 60 to 240 percent a year. Many of these contracts provided that a certain sum was to be paid on a certain date, but that if the debt were not discharged as prescribed, it was to bear interest of from 5.0 to 20 percent a month until paid. A number of such contracts were carried out, but finally legal opposition was made and in 1824 it was decided by the Supreme Court of Alabama that the interest on contracts of this kind was in the nature of a penalty and hence illegal. This ruling protected those who had not already paid, but those who had paid were in another situation. When they applied for relief, the court decided in 1827 that a statute of limitations barred the recovery of money which had already been paid out under such contracts.[5]

Although the issue was a purely legal matter, it was turned into a political question chiefly by William Kelly who, having failed to be re-elected to the Senate in 1824, had returned to the legislature and was counsel for a number of those persons seeking to recover money paid out under the "big-interest" contracts. Whereas the judges had been very popular because of their decision of 1824, a cry was now raised against them. They were accused of being enemies of the people and in league with the money-lenders. The old cry against the "Royal Party" of Huntsville was revived and there was said to be a "Radical Party" in the south which was the counterpart of the northern royalists. This party supposedly was not made up of any section of the public, but of a small group of men in the legislature—the old guard of the Crawford faction—who were working for their own interest. The Huntsville *Democrat* presented its view of the situation at some length:

In no county in the State, has the spirit of local partyism raged with equal violence as in Madison County. . . . But this local feeling has pervaded the whole state, in some counties quite covertly; while in others, it has burned with the utmost intensity. Some twelve or fifteen years ago, the Indian title to a large portion of Alabama was extinguished and straightway the tide of emigration set strongly towards this fertile territory. Persons flocked to it from all quarters; few of them wealthy—most from the expectation of bettering their fortunes. It was not to be presumed that a mass thrown thus loosely together could have pursued any systematic plan of internal policy, or have been actuated by anything like an identity of interests. It was consequently easy for an inconsiderable minority acting in concert, and with a determinate and well understood purpose to give tone to public sentiment, to carry their measures, and possess themselves of all valuable offices. Now, such a minority did exist in this state. They were chiefly composed of Georgians, who, from previous acquaintance, attachment to the civil institutions of Georgia, and a more than common portion of wealth, seemed to be connected together by a tie, the strength of which they all recognized by the support which they mutually extended to each other. . . . These circumstances inspired greater confidence, and led to such developments of their views as to create a distrust of that purity of character for which they had heretofore obtained credit. They evinced a determination to monopolize all power, and to fill every office with their own creatures. Many of these were so glaringly deficient in the requisite qualifications, that the people began to discover the "family" arrangements which were making to impose rulers over them. The yeomanry of this country, devotedly attached to Democratic principles, could but illy brook this assumption of superiority. . . . It is to Israel Pickens that the people are chiefly indebted for their dethronement; it was he who first broke the charm and showed that the Georgians with all their management and manoeuvering were not invincible.

Madison County was their great headquarters; here it was that the plan of operations was generally framed; and from thence communicated to their partisans throughout the State.

The article went on to say that these men had control of the Huntsville bank, and that they were responsible for the passage of the act abolishing interest limitations in 1818.[6]

In 1826 Henry Chambers died and the vacancy thus left in the Senate was filled by the appointment of Israel Pickens. But ill health forced Pickens to resign during the same year, and the election of a successor soon occupied the attention of the legislature. The opposing candidates were John McKinley, a wealthy lawyer from Florence, and Clement C. Clay, a prominent Huntsville attorney. Though Clay had been a member of the territorial council and is said to have voted for the fateful interest bill of 1818, and though he was at one time a stockholder in the Merchants' and Planters' Bank of Huntsville, he did not become identified with the capitalist group at Huntsville and seems to have been above reproach. In 1820 he became chief justice of the Supreme Court of Alabama, but resigned that position in 1823 to resume his legal practice.[7] This was his first appearance before the public since that time, and there seems to have been no reason why he should not have received the support of the popular party, but the Huntsville *Democrat* opposed him for reasons which are not evident and gave its support to McKinley, whom the same paper had opposed and labeled an aristocrat when he stood against Kelly for the Senate in 1822.[8]

That all this talk about party, though based upon certain concrete facts, was largely worked up for campaign purposes is indicated by an apparently candid statement made by McKinley shortly before the election of 1826.

I know nothing of the Royal Party or its policy, further than I have seen the subject discussed in the newspapers, and as far as comprehended by that discussion, I have no personal or political interest in it. I had been a citizen of this state about a year before I ever heard of the existence of a party in it. I was then informed by a friend, if I supported a particular individual for Governor, I would be considered as belonging to the *Georgia* party. What was meant by this party, I did not know, nor could my friend inform me as he was equally a stranger to its meaning or object. In 1821, I heard for the first time of the Royal party, and was equally at a loss to know what was the meaning of the name or the object of that party. In the fall of that year, I removed to this place where I heard but little more of parties until the fall of 1822, when I became a candidate for the same office for which I am now a candidate. When at the seat of government pending the election between Judge Kelly and myself, the charge of belonging to the Georgia party, Huntsville, and Royal party, was brought to bear upon my election. I had no mode of defending myself against the charge, but simply denying that I belonged to any party, which was the fact. In that contest I was beaten by a single vote, to which I submitted, I hope, with becoming propriety. I continued to reside in this place until February, 1825, without hearing my name connected with party, and having kept myself aloof from all party contests, had hoped to escape such an unfounded, and as I conceived, ungenerous imputation. But shortly after my return to Huntsville in the early part of 1825 this charge was revived against me, although I was a candidate for no office, nor took any active part in the local or general politics of the country. In the year 1823 a newspaper discussion took place in the *Democrat* and *Advocate* upon the subject of party, when it assumed a more tangible shape. The principal cause of complaint, as well as I now recollect, against what was termed the Royal party, was the statute of February, 1818, the combination of certain men to procure its passage, and the aid afforded by the Huntsville bank to those men to obtain funds to lend at exorbitant interest.[9]

This election, in which no question of policy was involved, and in which the two candidates seem to have been so nearly equal in fitness for popular leadership, was waged with so much bitterness of partisan feeling that it marks the point at which the popular party, having gained an undisputed ascendency, was becoming a prey to factious contests among its leaders. The struggle, though close, resulted in favor of McKinley.[10] (See figure 26.)

But Kelly and the *Democrat* did not intend to be without an issue of some sort. The fight against the Supreme Court judges was pressed. Kelly brought charges before the legislature against three of them on the plea that their decision of 1827 had gone counter to the precedent established by the cases of 1824 and that this was an improper application of law on their part. The complaint was not sustained, however, and the judges were exonerated by an overwhelming vote.[11] But the matter was not allowed to drop here. A constitutional amendment reducing judicial tenure from the period of good behavior to a term of six years was passed by the legislature in 1827; approved the next year by popular vote[12] (see figure 27), and incorporated as the first amendment to the state constitution in 1830.

FIGURE 26: House vote in election of U.S. Senator, 1826

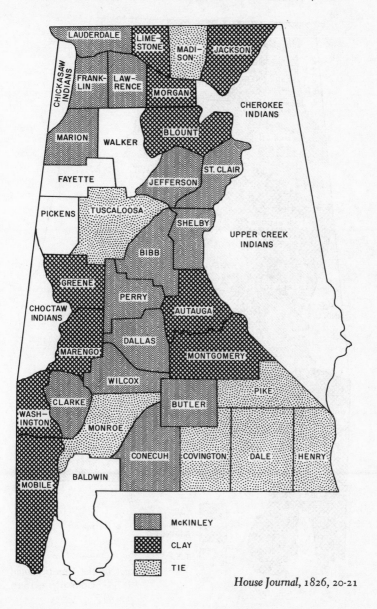

LAUDERDALE
LIME-STONE
MADI-SON
JACKSON
CHICKASAW INDIANS
FRANK-LIN
LAW-RENCE
MORGAN
CHEROKEE INDIANS
MARION
WALKER
BLOUNT
FAYETTE
ST. CLAIR
JEFFERSON
PICKENS
TUSCALOOSA
SHELBY
UPPER CREEK INDIANS
BIBB
GREENE
PERRY
CHOCTAW INDIANS
AUTAUGA
DALLAS
MARENGO
MONTGOMERY
WILCOX
CLARKE
PIKE
BUTLER
WASH-INGTON
MONROE
CONECUH
COVINGTON
DALE
HENRY
MOBILE
BALDWIN

McKINLEY
CLAY
TIE

House Journal, 1826, 20-21

FIGURE 27: Vote to reduce judicial tenure

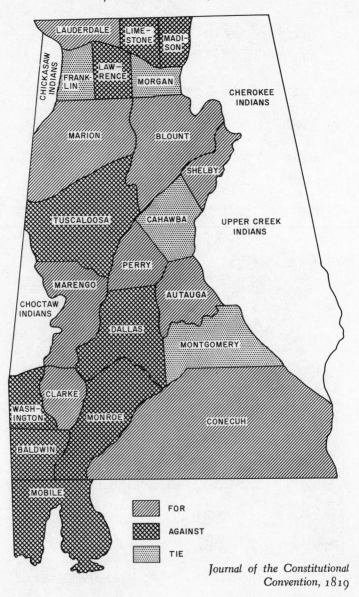

LAUDERDALE LIME-STONE MADI-SON

CHICKASAW INDIANS

FRANK-LIN LAW-RENCE MORGAN

CHEROKEE INDIANS

MARION BLOUNT

SHELBY

TUSCALOOSA CAHAWBA

UPPER CREEK INDIANS

PERRY

MARENGO AUTAUGA

CHOCTAW INDIANS

DALLAS

MONTGOMERY

CLARKE

WASH-INGTON MONROE

CONECUH

BALDWIN

MOBILE

FOR

AGAINST

TIE

Journal of the Constitutional
Convention, 1819

But while the disintegration of the Crawford faction after 1824 had deprived local politics of a real issue, national questions were coming more to the front. On some of these, such as the tariff, internal improvements, and slavery, the popular mind was well made up. On others, such as Indian policy and state rights, there was much more divergence of opinion. No one in the state had formulated any policies in regard to these questions, nor were there any political divisions along these lines. The legislature had to act from time to time on such questions, but the votes showed no definite alignments and seem to have been dictated by personal convictions or temporary considerations.

As to the tariff, there was a general and strong conviction that it was wrong to tax the agriculture of one section of the country for the benefit of the manufacturers of another. Yet there was a minority, led by the *Southern Advocate* and the supporters of Adams, which advocated a "competitive" tariff and insisted that the South must develop manufactures.

The interest of Alabama in the Muscle Shoals and the Coosa-Hiwassee canal projects, and the proposed road from Washington to New Orleans, brought about a general demand for internal improvements constructed with federal aid.[13] This threw the state astride on the question of state rights, for it was difficult to support improvements and denounce the tariff at the same time; and John Randolph and Nathaniel Macon were never tired of warning that to give the government the right to construct public works within the states would give it the right also to free the slaves.

This situation necessitated a certain amount of hedging when it became necessary to formulate general political doctrines, or to make out a case for favorite presidential aspirants. Before the election of 1828, Jackson was questioned as to his views and replied that they were the same as they had been in 1824 when he supported the tariff and internal improvement measures.[14] The friends of Adams stated that no distinction between the two men could be made on these grounds, and the contention, at this time, was at least reasonable. The preference for Jackson was personal, sectional, and democratic.

While the position of Alabama was not strictly logical according to the political schools of the time, it was practical and well-defined. Very little sympathy was extended to Troup while he was making his fight against the administration on the question of removal of the Creek Indians; and Georgia was roundly denounced for presuming that one state could upset the operations of the national government.[15] The prevalent opinion was that both Troup and Adams had behaved rashly; that the government was under obligation to remove the Indians from the state; and that Adams had blundered when he threatened to use federal troops to enforce his policy, just as Troup had erred in his attitude of uncompromising defiance. The original treaty with the Indians, which was later annulled and became the bone of contention, had secured a small tract of the Creek lands which lay within the limits of Alabama. Governor Murphy raised the question whether a third party could be deprived of rights under a contract even though it were not enforced as to the contracting parties.[16] The question was taken up in the legislature and a bill passed extending the jurisdiction of the state over the lands concerned.[17] But this was looked upon as merely the testing of a legal proposition, and the matter was carried no further.

A more severe strain upon the loyalty of the state came when the "tariff of abominations" was passed in 1828. There was universal dissatisfaction and even disgust with the policy pursued. It was felt that the interests of the cotton states were being sacrificed to the ambition of the manufacturing region and, whether it was wise, whether it was constitutional as the Constitution had originally been intended, there is no question that the planters were right as to the practical bearing of the situation. Protests went up on all sides; the development of home manufactures was urged, and the boycotting of imports, but it was always made clear that all resistance was to be peaceable. When forcible resistance was suggested or threatened in resolutions brought up before the legislature, the portentous clauses were stricken out by decisive votes.[18] Senator William R. King condemned the tariff in an address at Selma.

With a view, Gentlemen, to effect political objects, a systematic effort has been made to impress the belief upon the people of our country, that the high minded and patriotic inhabitants of the South and South West—the advocates and supporters of a most distinguished and meritorious citizen—are engaged in *planning the dissolution of our union; the destruction of this federative Government*—the legacy of our patriotic and sainted Fathers.[19]

On this occasion the following toasts were drunk: "The Union of the States—Palsied be the arm that shall be raised to sever it," and "The Tariff—Unconstitutional in principle, unjust and unequal in its operation—We will not oppose it with violence and passion, but by relying on our own resources."[20] The editor of the *Mobile Register*, referring to an address of the citizens of Colleton district, South Carolina, wrote: "We will frankly declare, it was not from the State of South Carolina that we ever expected a proposition the bare contemplation of which must cause the heart of a patriot to sink within him."[21]

But there was another movement on foot which led in a different direction and which was fraught with meaning for the future. This movement, though not original in conception, was a new influence in Alabama and it was important at that time only because its leader, who knew what he believed and where he was going, was able to fit his purpose to the material in hand and secure the temporary support of men who did not understand whither he was leading them. This new influence is interesting not only because of its significance for the future, but for its connection with the past.

Dixon H. Lewis was born in Dinwiddie County, Virginia, in 1802. His father was among those Virginians who moved to Georgia in the days when upland cotton was beginning to supplant tobacco as the main agricultural staple of the South. From Georgia he moved to Autauga County, Alabama, in 1820.[22]

Young Lewis studied law at Cahawba in the office of Henry Hitchcock, a New Englander who had come out to Alabama as secretary to the territorial governor, and who was now attorney general of the state. The political influence in the life of Lewis was exerted by his uncle, Bolling Hall, the Georgia congressman who had come to Alabama with Tait, Walker, and other supporters of Crawford. Hall was not only a friend of Crawford, but of Nathaniel Macon, John Taylor, and others who had long stood for strict construction of the Constitution.

The views of Lewis were essentially the views of these men, whom Alabama had heard from afar and ignored. But in 1826 the energetic young lawyer won a spirited election in Montgomery County and went up to the legislature to make his debut in politics. He had not been there more than twenty-four hours when he drew up a set of resolutions condemning the exercise of implied, constructive, and unconstitutional powers on the part of the federal government, and had it presented to the Senate by his friend, Matt Clay. These resolutions were passed with only one dissenting vote after the following clause had been stricken:

> Resolved, That we believe the time has again arrived when it is necessary for the States to assert their constitutional rights, and with becoming firmness to resist the increasing progress of federal power.[23]

In pursuance of his views Lewis took up the Indian question and in 1828 presented a report in the House of Representatives in which it was argued that the state had jurisdiction over the natives within her borders and that the United States had no right to interfere between them.[24] Along with the report he presented a bill proposing to extend the jurisdiction of the state over the Creeks, and though almost every member of the House at first disapproved the idea, the measure was finally passed, receiving most of its support from the counties bordering the Creek reservation.[25] (See Figure 28.)

But it was not only on national questions that Lewis had convictions. He had inherited from Bolling Hall and the Crawford men a sincere dislike of the state bank and, though at this time the foundations of that institution were unassailable, he began to attack it at vulnerable points. There had been a noisy contest in

FIGURE 28: Vote on bill to extend jurisdiction
of state over Creeks

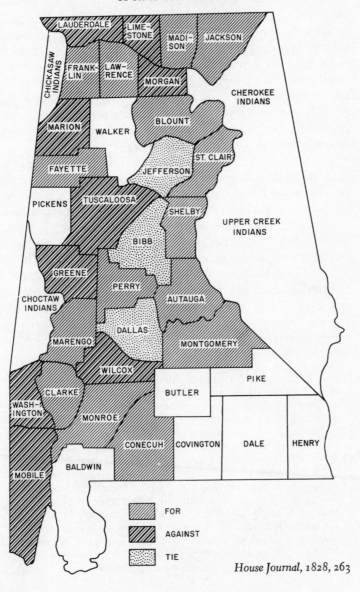

FOR

AGAINST

TIE

House Journal, 1828, 263

the legislature over the question as to whether that body was permitted to inspect the private accounts of the bank. The cashier refused to show the private books to the visiting committee and the opponents of the institution at once raised their voices in protest. They apparently failed in their attempt to cast discredit upon the management. The procedure of Lewis was less spectacular, but more to the point.[26] The legislature was in the habit of levying taxes in excess of disbursements and using the balance for banking purposes. It was this practice which Lewis now attacked and succeeded in stopping.[27]

The attitude of the new leader on the question of the state bank brings out his connection with the earlier opponents of the popular party but the manner in which political ground had shifted is shown by the fact that when resolutions proposing Jackson for the presidency were to be brought before the legislature in 1827, it was Lewis who was chosen to present them.

After condemning the existing administration because it had departed from the principle of strict construction, because it had accepted internal improvements as a fixed policy and one destructive of state sovereignty, because of its attitude on the Panama mission, and because it had adopted the policy of encouraging one industry at the expense of another by prohibitory duties, the resolution said:

Another prominent act of Mr. Adams requires particular notice, viz: his threat to employ military force against one of the sovereign members of the confederacy. So great a want of temper, such an entire misconception of the character of the American people, and so extraordinary a claim to power is believed to be unparalleled in the history of any preceding administration. More forbearance might have been expected from a prince of unlimited powers to one of the most rebellious provinces of his dominion. Before any negotiation of a friendly character was attempted, or even a measure of compromise proposed, the State of Georgia was threatened with the military force of the Union for the purpose of forcing her into an unconstitutional abandonment of substantial rights of sovereignty, secured to her by the solemn stipulation of treaty—This State cannot but share some portion of the responsibility thrown upon Georgia in this matter, inasmuch as an enactment of the last legislature, and a resolution of the same body recognized the principles for which Georgia was then contending. As Alabamians, therefore, the committee feels bound to protest against this violent measure of the President of the United States. . . . To counteract so powerful an influence, a systematic effort is required of the people, and a concentration of their entire strength on some distinguished individual.[28]

General Jackson was named as that individual and the resolutions passed by a vote of fifty-four to eight, but they do not represent the kind of Jacksonism which was characteristic of the earlier supporters of the General. The young lawyer from Montgomery had a remarkable faculty for bringing the legislature to his way of thinking when he did not have strong convictions to overcome, and here was a fine denunciation of Adams. It was gladly accepted because it served the purpose in hand, and no one thought it worthwhile to criticize its purely negative support of Jackson and its very positive support of state rights, to which the majority of the people did not subscribe.

Though Adams electors were nominated, the General carried the state almost without opposition[29] and soon entered upon the administration that was to see the birth of questions which would divide his followers. In Alabama, under the leadership of Lewis, the planters were to add a plea for the safety of the slave states to their old distrust of mass government, and to divide the commonwealth into two distinct, well-defined, and fairly-balanced parties.

CHAPTER THIRTEEN

Religion, Education, and the Press

THE PRESS CAME INTO ALABAMA WITH THE SET-
tlers and exercised a strong influence during the formative period
of the state. The little four-page sheets which came out once or
twice a week were largely taken up with advertisements and
notices. A crude system of classifying advertisements enabled the
reader to select readily those in which he was interested. This was
accomplished by inserting a small cut indicative of the subject-
matter: a picture of a tree, for instance, would indicate that the
advertiser had land for sale; a cut of a house would show that
buildings were for rent or sale; while a Negro with a bundle
swung over his shoulder at the end of a stick would proclaim the
escape of a slave.

That portion of the paper, usually amounting to less than two
of the four pages, which was devoted to the news was principally
taken up with extracts from the leading papers of the older
states. Many of these articles related to political affairs, but
foreign news, though much belated, received considerable attention. A florid style was typical of the press of that day, and words
were used with especial freedom when a political subject claimed
the attention of the editor or contributor. Indeed, it seems to
have been the universal practice to treat a political opponent as
a moral or mental delinquent.

The editors of Alabama papers confined their remarks to one or two columns, where they expressed their opinions upon national politics or subjects of local interest. Personal affairs were never paraded in print, nor was mention ever made of social activities. This was due not only to ideas of decorum which differ from modern ones, but also to the conception that the press was strictly a public institution. Letters from subscribers on political matters were frequently published, and these formed an important element in every discussion.

The first newspaper published in that part of the Mississippi Territory which was soon to become Alabama was the *Mobile Centinel,* established at Fort Stoddert in 1811 while Mobile was still Spanish territory.[1] It maintained a precarious existence for less than two years, and was hardly more than a patriotic gesture. The real beginning of Alabama journalism came with the founding of the *Madison Gazette,* first published in Huntsville in 1812. In 1816 its name was changed to the *Alabama Republican*[2] and in 1825 it was consolidated with the *Alabamian* to become the *Southern Advocate.*[3] John Boardman, a Massachusetts man who allied himself with the "Aristocratic Party" of Huntsville, was editor, first of the *Republican,* and later of the *Advocate.* He supported Adams for the presidency in 1824 and, though going over to Jackson in 1828, he always opposed the state bank and its adherents.

In 1823 an opposition paper called the *Democrat* was founded at Huntsville.[4] Its editor, William B. Long of Kentucky, was a supporter of Clay. Claiming to be a leader of "the people" as opposed to "the aristocracy" and the *Alabama Republican,* he hotly took issue with Boardman on the question of the state bank, and presently came over to the support of Jackson for the presidency. Crawford men, the Merchants' and Planters' Bank of Huntsville, and "aristocrats" in general were the particular antipathies of the *Democrat;* at the same time it was lenient toward those who combined the support of the state bank with that of Adams. So bitter was its attitude toward its opponents that Long's successor, Andrew Wills, who had come from Virginia to Huntsville as a school teacher, was shot down on the street by a political enemy.

The storm center of Alabama was in the Tennessee Valley, and the *Democrat* and the *Republican* expressed the extreme views of the two factions. In the remainder of the state there was less agitation, the interior towns usually having but one paper which, while expressing its own views, took a mild attitude in order to retain the goodwill of all moderate men.

In Mobile commercial affairs were given precedence over politics. The first paper published here—the *Mobile Gazette*—was established in 1816 by George B. Cotten.[5] In 1821, John Battelle, having established the *Montgomery Republican* in the same year, formed a partnership with J. W. Townsend and founded the *Mobile Commercial Register*.[6] John Battelle was a native of Boston and a member of the Alabama Company which helped to found the town of Montgomery. The *Register* supported Crawford for the presidency, and in 1822 it bought out the *Gazette*,[7] a move which its enemies attributed to political motives. Its principal interest was in commercial affairs, and it opposed the establishment of a state bank according to the plan advocated by Pickens. In 1822, the *Mobile Argus* was founded by Charles A. Henry,[8] but the following year the firm of Nicholas and Henry succeeded to the ownership and changed the name to the *Mercantile Advertiser*.[9] This paper supported Adams for the presidency, but like practically all others of that faith, it claimed "to do justice to all."

Battelle's *Montgomery Republican* changed its name in 1825 to the *Montgomery Journal*.[10] It supported Adams from the first. The *Cahawba Press*, founded in 1819 at the state capital by William B. Allen,[11] a native of Boston, joined the support of Adams with that of Pickens and the state bank. In 1824 Allen sold his paper to Thomas P. Lumpkin, but when the purchaser proceeded to support Crawford, the friends of the state bank, both Jackson and Adams men, combined to set Allen up in business again and to give a new lease on life to the *Press*.[12] The fact that Allen, despite the competition of Lumpkin and others, was elected state printer as long as the capital remained at Cahawba, shows that the support of Adams was not particularly detrimental to the popularity of an editor so long as he was a friend of "the people's Bank."[13]

In 1819, there were six papers in Alabama: the *Alabama Republican* of Huntsville, the *Halcyon* (established at St. Stephens in 1814), the *Mobile Gazette*, the *Cahawba Press*, the *Blakely Sun*, and the *American Mirror* of Tuscaloosa. By 1823 the number had risen to ten,[14] and the next year it amounted to fifteen.[15] During 1825, there were sixteen or seventeen papers published in the state,[16] but the following year saw the number reduced again to ten.[17]

The great publishing activity of 1824 was undoubtedly a result of the presidential campaign of that year, and it speaks much for the political influence of the press at that time. In 1824 it was said that, of the fifteen papers in Alabama, seven, edited by northern men, were for Adams; but all of these except the Huntsville *Republican*, were published in the southern part of the state.[18] Two years later, when the number of papers had been reduced to ten and the support of Jackson had become almost universal among the people, three publications were said to have remained steadfast in their support of Adams, three or four were said to have opposed him consistently, while the rest maintained an uncertain attitude.[19] The popularity of the New Englander in the Alabama press can be ascribed primarily to the northern origin of so many of the editors. The combination of the support of Pickens and the state bank with that of Adams increased the popularity of publications which differed from the majority of their patrons on the subject of the presidency. Nevertheless, there was a tendency among the newspaper men to modify their opinions gradually in order to accommodate themselves to the trend of public sentiment.

The early settlers of Alabama were not indifferent to the problem of education, and the grant of the sixteenth section in each township for local schools afforded a solid foundation upon which to build, but the results were not as favorable as might have been expected. In good agricultural districts, the sixteenth section usually yielded sufficient income to support, or partially support, several schools with fairly well-paid teachers. But in areas where the soil was poor, there was little income from the land, and the zeal of the population was usually not sufficient to make up the deficit.[20] Travelers noted the existence of creditable free schools as early as 1820,[21] but these were not universal —perhaps not even usual.

One of the main difficulties lay in the management of the school property. This was vested in a board of commissioners appointed by the county authorities.[22] Supervision over these commissions was vague or non-existent, and their conduct of affairs was a frequent source of complaint.[23]

Even such support as the public schools possessed was menaced when the strong appeal of the state bank induced the legislature to promote a scheme for selling the sixteenth sections and investing the proceeds in the popular institution. In 1826, the Alabama delegation was instructed by the legislature to secure from Congress permission to sell these lands and devote the proceeds to the maintenance of the schools.[24] In 1827, Congress granted the request, providing that the sale should be made only with the consent of the township concerned.[25] The next year the legislature made provisions for carrying out the plan. The proceeds of the lands were to be invested in the state bank at 6.0 percent interest and the income devoted to the purpose for which the grant had been made.[26] Thus the bank could look forward to a considerable extension of its resources, and the schools could contemplate an uncertain future.

In addition to the public schools, private schools were established from time to time in the larger towns, and by 1823 as many as eight academies had been chartered.[27] Apparently, the first of these to go into actual operation was *Green Academy*, chartered by the legislature of the Mississippi Territory in 1812. Though a grant of $500 was made to this institution in 1816 and funds provided at a later date brought the total up to about

$2,000, nothing had been done toward putting the school in operation before 1820.[28] At about this time, however, the trustees bestirred themselves, raised funds by popular subscription, and had a creditable institution in operation within a year or two.[29]

The first academy for girls was founded at Athens in 1822, and appears to have been a successful enterprise.[30] At about the same time, a private school for girls was opened in Huntsville by a Mr. and Mrs. DeVendel.

The subjects usually taught during this period included grammar, history, mathematics, and geography, while the schools for girls also included in their curriculum music, needle-work, painting, and dancing. The academies took up instruction in Latin, some of the sciences, and rhetoric.

The federal government had granted two townships to the State of Alabama for the purpose of founding a university, and in 1819 that institution was given a formal recognition by the legislature, but nothing more than a name was established at this time.[31] In 1821 a board of trustees was appointed and given power to dispose of the university lands, invest the proceeds and establish the institution as soon as a site should be designated by the legislature.[32] The first meeting of the board was held during the next year and arrangements were made for disposing of the property. It was decided to adopt a credit system of sales, requiring one-fourth of the purchase money to be paid down, and the remainder to be paid in three installments.[33] During the first few years there was a brisk demand for the lands, and by 1828 the total sales amounted to $285,000.[34]

But the state bank interfered here also and the establishment of the University was delayed. The trustees could not move until the legislature had decided on the location, and Governor Pickens, being anxious to use the university funds as capital for the bank, secured the postponement of the location until after his term of office had expired.[35] It was intended from the first that the greater part of the fund should be used as an endowment, and considering the hopes that were entertained for the success of the bank, there was nothing morally wrong in the governor's plan for investment, but his attitude shows where his interest chiefly lay. About $89,000, or practically all the cash received in payment on the lands sold, was invested by the trustees of the University in the bank before anything was done to give the institution of learning a practical existence.[36]

Governor Murphy, on coming into office, advised the legislature to locate the University,[37] and in 1827 Tuscaloosa was selected as its site.[38] In 1828 the trustees drew up a plan including the construction of the following buildings: one central structure to be used as a chapel, lecture hall, and library; one chemical laboratory and lecture hall; four professors' houses, each accommodating two professors; two or more hotels or boarding houses; and six dormitories. It was proposed that the central building, the laboratory, two of the professors' houses, one hotel, and two dormitories be erected at once, and contracts were let accordingly.[39] A tract of fifty acres adjoining the University site was purchased so that clay for brick and timber for structural purposes could be obtained close at hand.[40] The cornerstone was laid during the same year,[41] and in 1831 the University of Alabama opened its doors, with Dr. Alva Woods, formerly head of Transylvania University, as its first president.[42]

In religious matters, the Methodists and Baptists have always held the center of the field in Alabama. The predominance of these two denominations in the old Southwest is an interesting phenomenon, and the development in one state would probably be paralleled by the situation in most of the others.

The period following the American Revolution was a fertile one for the sowing of religious seed. The events of the French Revolution had left the world more or less in doubt concerning its old creeds, and the French philosophers, followed by Jefferson and Franklin in the United States, gave skepticism a wide vogue. But the visits of John Wesley and George Whitefield had earlier brought a new faith, and at a time when America was beginning to spread westward.

The organization of the Methodist society was peculiarly fitted to frontier conditions. With a central governing body made up of the bishops, a definite policy could be adopted and carried out in an effective manner. With its "free-for-all" ideas regarding the ministry, men could be drawn into the service of the church whose lack of education was atoned for by a zeal which strengthened them to endure the hardships of the wilderness and to work for the love of their creed with little compensation in a material way. The institution of the circuit rider enabled one man to do the work of several and was a most efficient means of coping with frontier conditions. Finally the development of the "camp meeting" brought the scattered people together under conditions which had a strong emotional appeal to the pioneer and enabled a few men to exert a powerful influence over many.[43]

In the combination of these means, the Methodists had an advantage over all other denominations in the thinly-settled frontier; but the Baptists, though lacking organization, had a zeal which largely overcame this difficulty. Their appeal, like that of the Methodists, was to the emotions of the plain man, and their ministry was also adapted to frontier conditions. They brought their gospel to the pioneer by much the same means as those employed by the followers of Wesley, and the local independence of their churches seems to have been so agreeable to the free spirit of the West that it enabled them to compete on equal terms with their religious rivals.

In the early part of the nineteenth century, religion was neither accepted nor rejected with the indifference that it is accorded today. The average backwoodsman was not by nature inclined to be strictly religious, but he was inclined to be positive. When the question came to him he took his stand either for or against it, and made a good supporter or an outspoken antagonist. Neither was he inclined to be theoretical, and in the struggle between the Methodists and the Baptists, he seems to have been more interested in the spirit in which the rivals worked than in their rival creeds.

But all this does not apply to the planters. It was said that the cultured people never went to camp meetings[44] at which there were displays of crude, effervescent emotionalism often repulsive to the more refined. The strongholds of the Methodists and Baptists were in the rural districts.[45] Townspeople were apparently more or less unfamilar with camp meeting procedures as is indicated by a description which the editor of the Huntsville *Democrat,* who was a defender of religion, thought it worthwhile to print.

A favorable spot in the woods was selected as the place of worship, and a crude pulpit and altar was erected. Benches were arranged around this, and tents for the accommodation of tables and guests were pitched about the grounds. Two sermons were usually preached in the morning, and then a short recess was allowed for dinner. At this time, the worshippers would repair to the tents where abundant supplies of food were laid out for the benefit of all. People from the surrounding country came on horseback, in carriages, or afoot, as circumstances permitted, bringing their picnic lunches with them. The occasion was one of social as well as religious enjoyment, and crowds of thousands were sometimes assembled to hear favorite exhorters. After dinner, the services were resumed, and they were always concluded by an invitation to repentant sinners to come up to the altar. Large numbers usually went forward, and as the minister prayed for them, the congregation went into a religious ecstacy of praying, moaning, and shouting. But it must not be inferred that these were disorderly gatherings. There was a spirit of sociability and festivity on the part of the people and of gravity on the part of the leaders which gave them a dignity of their own.[46]

The planters usually had at least some latent religious belief. There were Episcopalians among them, but they were not of a missionary spirit and their numbers were too few to found many churches in the early days.[47] Presbyterians were present in larger numbers and a church of that faith was usually established in the leading towns.[48] Here they were active rivals of the Methodists and Baptists, who also established churches and held "protracted" meetings.[49] Bible societies were organized in several places,[50] and Huntsville had an interdenominational Sunday school.[51] In Mobile the Episcopalians formed the nucleus of an interdenominational protestant church, which was the only rival of the older Catholic congregation there.[52]

CHAPTER FOURTEEN

Social Conditions and Slavery

IN A NEWLY-SETTLED AREA TO WHICH PEOPLE have flocked from many places and for many purposes, one would expect to find varied social conditions, and in Alabama they ran all the way from one extreme to the other. To begin at the bottom, the Indian border offered a favorite location for fugitives from justice, traffickers in whisky, and rascals of every description. The state had no jurisdiction within the reservation, a fact which was taken advantage of by this element. It worked a great hardship on the natives and gave rise to complaints which were fully justified, but very hard to rectify.[1] It was often said that the contact between the red men and the white men was sadly detrimental to the former, and since their associations were usually with the worst of the whites, this is not hard to understand.

But the miscreants were not confined to the borders. New country is attractive to adventurers of every sort; the lonely roads through the forests afforded robbers a choice field of operations, while the towns were alluring to gamblers of various breeds.[2] There is an account of a band of men, intercepted on their way to Huntsville, whose baggage was found to contain counterfeit notes and gambling devices of every description.[3] Complaints were made that gamesters in that town often assumed an air of importance because they were noticed by prominent men[4] among whom the young often seem to have fallen easy prey to the wandering gamblers.[5]

The towns were infested also with people who were not criminals, but who might be termed "rowdy."[6] While the young men of the towns appear to have been dandyish, inclined toward idleness and gambling rather than to boorishness,[7] the rowdies seemed to have been visitors from the surrounding country who came to town for a boisterous holiday. It is stated that in Greensboro horseracing through the main street became such a nuisance that the citizens threatened to shoot anyone who persisted in the practice.[8]

It was, however, at the crossroads store, the militia muster, and the barbecue that the rustics mostly congregated. Horseplay was the rule at such places, and assemblies usually ended in drunkenness and fighting. Yet these frays were not so much blood-thirsty affairs, as just a hardy form of sport. Those who engaged in them were not brutal, but merely vigorous pioneers who loved a struggle with nature or with man.[9]

The barbecue, like the camp meeting, was an institution. Its use was largely political and its appeal seems to have been almost irresistible. Before an election, barbecues were arranged and advertised by men interested in making money from them. Shoat and whisky in abundance were always taken for granted, and the candidates were bound to appear, to assert their claims and prove their belief in democracy.[10] Sentiment against the barbecues began to be aroused about 1826, at which time the Huntsville papers instituted a campaign against them. The candidates seem to have been willing enough to drop the practice, and some began to refrain from attendance.[11] But whisky was always one of the strongest persuaders in a political campaign. A Mobile paper published an ironical offer to furnish any man enough whisky to drown his reason on election day, which was a jibe at the custom of "treating" by the candidates.[12] A Huntsville paper makes the statement that bottles of liquor were arranged in rows with labels on them which the casual observer would take for designations of brand, but which in reality named the candidate who furnished the drink.[13]

This is the darker side of a picture which was not all dark.

The habit of drinking was almost universal at the time, and the practice of "treating" was looked upon more as hospitality than as bribery. But the people of early Alabama farmed their patches of cotton and corn, lived a hardy, rugged life close to nature, were friendly toward their neighbors and hospitable toward strangers, made an honest living for themselves and their families, attended to their own business most of the time and only rarely had leisure to celebrate.[14]

The planters formed a society to themselves, yet it was neither closed nor homogeneous. The less affluent planters lived much as did the farmers, while those with extensive estates sometimes attained an elegance which was impressive. The great majority of them, however, were merely in comfortable circumstances and their pride was based not upon wealth or display, but upon the sense of independence and authority which their position in society gave them.

Perhaps Montgomery County best represents the planter life of the early days. The soil here was more uniformly fertile than that of most other counties, and consequently it was settled mostly by planters. Prosperity and independence came to be the rule. Because of easy water communication with Mobile and business on a sufficiently large scale to warrant it, the planters had few dealings with local merchants, but traded directly with the Gulf port, generally going down once a year to purchase supplies. The sociability of the people and the law-abiding nature of the community were apparently ideal, since a jail was not maintained and only one duel was fought during the early period.[15]

It is true that the combination of rural simplicity and native refinement on the plantation at its best furnished the basis for a picturesque and pleasant civilization, but the best was not often attained. In Madison County, for instance, there was a large planting community, but some of the planters were excessively wealthy and used their wealth to secure commercial and political advantages. This aroused the antagonism of men who were not financially independent, among whom there was a strong element of Tennessee farmers willing to wage the fight. In spite of the general tendency for the poor to be jealous of the rich, there was no antagonism against the planters as such.[16] The plainer people had no political leaders of their own and appear to have been perfectly willing to support planters of means when they made it their business to court favor by advocating popular measures.

The social atmosphere of Alabama established by the planters varied from place to place. Where wealth was evenly distributed and notable fortunes and town life were largely lacking, there does not appear to have been that gaiety of social intercourse which is usually attributed to plantation life. The people spent their time in an unassuming and largely self-sufficient way. But neighborliness and hospitality were not wanting even under these circumstances.[17] Gaiety was the rule, however, in the towns which furnished the centers of recreation.[18] Dramatic clubs were formed among the young people, theaters were built in the larger communities, and dances and parties were of frequent occurrence. There was a greater freedom in Western society than in that of the East;[19] calling was more informal and women were somewhat less restricted by convention. An Eastern paper criticized the ladies of Huntsville for attending a Fourth of July celebration at the local inn, and a local editor defended them, saying that he saw nothing improper in their action.[20] There was a general diffusion of information concerning matters of common knowledge, but though libraries were established in Huntsville and Montgomery, as a rule little attention was paid to purely intellectual cultivation. Among the men, horseracing was a favorite sport and courses were established in the vicinity of the more important towns. Some fanciers had fast English bred horses and kept race tracks of their own. Playing for stakes was a common diversion and drinking was as prevalent among the wealthy as it was among the poor. It is stated in the biography of James G. Birney that while living in Huntsville, he followed the fashion in all these things,[21] and the historian of the Baptist denomination in Alabama asserts that even ministers were often fond of the bottle and carried potions of their favorite brands in their pockets when they went to meetings.[22] But gentlemen prided themselves on knowing when they had had enough. As always, the earliest days were the roughest. A settler of this period who had not attended a trial in many years was so impressed by the improved order which he found in the courtroom after his long absence, that he said he felt as though he were attending church services.[23]

The conditions under which slavery adjusted itself to a new frontier afford an interesting topic for study, but, since matters of domestic economy were taken for granted, specific information is difficult to obtain, and no Alabama accounts of slavery during the earliest period have been located.

Captain Basil Hall gives an excellent description of the plantation system of "tasking" as it existed on a sea-island estate of Georgia in 1828,[24] and E. C. Holland, in a treatise written on the subject in 1822 says that this was the universal practice.[25] The hands, were rated in accordance with their physical ability and given daily "tasks" in proportion to their strength. The fields were staked off into half-acre, or three-quarter-acre tracts, and one, two, or three of these tracts, depending upon the nature of the work to be done, constituted the task for the day. Diligence enabled the slave to finish his assignment early in the afternoon and he was allowed to spend the remainder of the day at leisure. In this way discipline was maintained, the necessity for compulsion was reduced to a minimum, and the slave was given a stimulus to work.

Hall states that this tasking system was universally employed, noting that the existence of distinct classes in the South discouraged all innovation, and scattered references to it appear in agricultural discussions. Writers of the period stress the necessity for well-defined and clearly-understood regulations in the management of slaves, and the insistence on strict enforcement of discipline.[26] The disgruntled slave had the recourse of running away, and in order to prevent this and secure effective organization, regularity, kindness, and firmness were essential.

When the system was transplanted to the new soil of Alabama, differences in spirit, if not in form, would necessarily arise; but the available information is too scant to allow a thorough study of the changes. The provisions for slavery which were incorporated in the constitution of 1819 were of a liberal spirit. Slaves might be freed by their owners with the consent of the legislature, or the legislature might take the initiative in liberating Negroes provided the consent of their owners had been obtained, or remuneration made. In addition, slaves were not to be deprived of trial by petit jury when arraigned for crimes more serious than petty larceny; and in case a slave were murdered or dismembered, the punishment for the crime was to be the same as though a white man had been the victim. The provisions show a desire to treat the unfortunate race with consideration, but the problem of managing slaves was a delicate one, and difficulties developed. The Negroes were irresponsible and often faithless. When they were displeased, they frequently ran away and lodged in swamps to prey upon the surrounding country. When they were allowed to go at large on Sundays, they congregated in the towns and became a public nuisance. When they were allowed to hire out their own time, they often became idlers in the streets. When they were allowed to sell the produce of their leisure hours, they often stole and sold the property of their masters.[27] In order to remedy this situation, acts were passed forbidding slaves to sell any articles except such simple things as they could make with their own hands.[28] Passes were required of Negroes who wished to visit premises belonging to others than their masters,[29] and in order to prevent slaves from wandering around the country or holding unauthorized meetings where dangerous doctrines might be inculcated, a patrol system was kept up. Military districts were established, all able-bodied men were required to serve in the militia, and the captain of each company was required to detail patrols whose duty it was to enforce the law.[30] But the administration of the system was frequently lax, and it therefore lacked effectiveness.

Slavery was, at this period, looked upon by southerners as a necessary evil and the slave trader was heartily detested by the planters in general.[31] This spirit found its expression in Alabama through an act of the legislature in 1826 which forbade the introduction of slaves for purposes of sale.[32] It is apparent, too, that this move was prompted by the depressed state of the cotton market which accompanied the panic of 1825, and which caused many to feel that overproduction of the staple would result from an increase in the number of laborers.[33] But in this matter, Alabama was merely following the lead of most of the other cotton-producing states.

The question of slavery was open to debate in the South until the activity of the Abolitionists and the Nat Turner insurrection in Virginia convinced the planters that agitation was dangerous to their system and their safety.[34] James G. Birney, who was a resident of Huntsville during these years, was instrumental in the enactment of the lenient provisions in regard to slavery which have been mentioned, and his biographer states that his ideas were not in advance of the sentiment of the planters of that day.[35] Opinions deprecating the existence of slavery were printed by some of the editors who published papers in Alabama,[36] and in 1824 the Tuscaloosa *Mirror* advertised that subscriptions to Benjamin Lundy's pioneer abolitionist paper, the *Genius of Universal Emancipation* would be received at the office of the local publication.[37] In discussing a memorial from the legislature of Ohio, which advocated general emancipation, the governor of Alabama spoke mildly and said that an offer of remuneration by the government might some day be opportune.[38]

The first sign of a defensive attitude on the part of Alabamians appeared when the legislature attempted in 1827 to pass an act forbidding the teaching of slaves by free persons. Though receiving the support of a good part of the southern portion of the state, the measure was defeated by the opposition which it encountered in the Tennessee Valley.[39]

This was the only instance in which any degree of sectionalism was betrayed during the 'twenties concerning the question of slavery in Alabama. Even in the vote on the bill to prohibit the

FIGURE 29: Vote on bill to prohibit importing slaves for sale

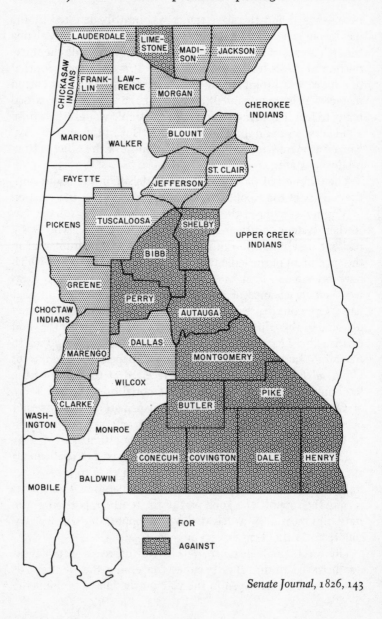

further introduction of slaves for sale, there was no alignment of slaveholding against non-slaveholding counties. The Tennessee Valley and the Alabama-Tombigbee valleys were the principal cotton-producing areas, but this fact would never be discovered by a study of the votes. (See Figure 29.) There were some planters who thought that enough slaves had already been introduced, while there were farmers who expected some day to purchase slaves and become planters themselves. Such a situation emphasizes the fact that there was no class antagonism between the cotton planter and the small farmer.

In the Tennessee Valley there were a few estates numbering several hundred slaves, but the majority of men who came to Alabama were in moderate circumstances. It was not those who had made their fortunes, but those who sought to make them, who were willing to sever the old ties and move into the new country. Twenty or thirty Negroes seem to have been a normal force for the average estate, but the majority of men who emigrated to Alabama had, it would seem, fewer than that.

The early history of Alabama appears to have been deeply influenced by the relatively close contact between the planters and the farmers. The frontier conditions which threw men upon their own resources and promoted rapid changes in station; the relatively narrow extent of the cotton-producing areas and the consequent proximity of planting and farming districts; the moderate estates of the planters and the lack of exclusive society outside the largest towns; the relatively small number of planters as compared with the farmers—all these conditions made Alabama a state where democracy was the rule in spite of slavery.

CHAPTER FIFTEEN

Conclusion

WHEN ONE ATTEMPTS TO TRACE THE ECONOMIC and political development of Alabama during the formative period, he must point out those factors which appear to him to have had special significance. We begin with a country which contained only one white settlement isolated in the midst of Indian tribes. The native had long dreaded the continued intrusion of the white man, and the effects of the unwelcome contact were telling upon him in several important ways. The sturdy self-reliance which the wilderness had instilled in him was being undermined by a state of semi-dependence, while whisky and the sharpers who sold it to him were combining to degrade his natural honesty. But the white man was striking at the roots of his existence in another way. As his land was taken from him bit by bit, the problem of living by the chase became ever more difficult. It was already impossible to rely altogether upon game for subsistence, and all the southern Indians engaged in primitive agriculture, the agents sent among them by the government doing all they could to promote the industry by the introduction of new crops and improved methods. But the red man looked ahead and adopted one of two policies for his future. He either strove to adapt himself to the conditions of civilization, or he assumed an attitude of hostile resistance to the invasion of the whites.

The white men who pushed ahead of civilization into the Ala-

bama region came partly as traders and partly as settlers. Some
of the traders took up their abode among the Indians and chose
native wives. Those who came for agricultural purposes gathered
upon the lower Tombigbee, where the land had been cleared
of the Indian title. Some of them used large numbers of slaves in
the culture of indigo and cotton, while others raised great herds
of cattle which roamed throughout the year in the canebrakes.
English, Scottish, and American blood was mixed with that of
the Indians in this crude frontier society.

When the War of 1812 was over, when the Creeks had been
defeated by Jackson and new lands were thrown open to settlement, squatters rushed in ahead of the government sales. The
best lands were put on the market first, and by the time they
were offered at public auction, the high price of cotton had
created a feverish demand for these tracts. Currency disorders
added to the excitement of speculation, and the result was that
the actual settlers, who were usually men without means, could
not compete for possession. It was during the years 1817, 1818,
and 1819, that the boom rose and fell, and the cotton kingdom
was started in Alabama. The planters from the very beginning
took the river valleys for their own, but the prairie region, situated just south of Montgomery and Tuscaloosa and joining the
upper Alabama basin with that of the Black Warrior, was not
extensively settled until the 'thirties, With this exception, the
cotton-producing areas were marked out during the period of first
settlement. The men who were not wealthy enough to own slaves
or to purchase the most desirable cotton lands took up their
abode in the back country, which offered fertile though isolated
fields. Here they were usually able to purchase their farms at the
minimum of $1.25 an acre, the prevailing price after the specu-
lative period ended. Thus there was not a great deal of active
competition between the two agricultural classes for the purchase
of lands, and circumstances effected such a distribution of the
territory between them that no general readjustment was ever
necessary. It is true that the percentage of slaves in Alabama
gradually increased, but the only counties in which the growth

was marked were in the prairie region, which had not been extensively settled by men of the farming class.

The outstanding economic factor during the period of settlement was the condition of indebtedness which applied to the community as a whole. Money was in great demand for investment in lands and slaves, and though the production of cotton brought in considerable funds, much was reinvested in agricultural equipment and a large part went for supplies of flour, corn, and pork. So great was the interest in cotton planting that it was quite difficult to secure capital for other business. The result was that merchandising was left largely to men from the northern states, while banking had to be carried on either by those who were able to secure special privileges through their operations, or by the state.

While the planter who operated on a large scale could deal directly with Mobile or New Orleans and thereby render himself largely independent of country merchants and bankers, the small farmer, dependent upon a local market and a disordered currency, was at a disadvantage in financial transactions. The distance from New Orleans to the Tennessee Valley region, and the questionable transactions of the Merchants' and Planters' Bank of Huntsville rendered this situation particularly acute, and promoted a class antagonism between the small farmers, predominantly of Tennessee origin, and the Georgia financiers and their associates. It was out of this antagonism that partisan differences first arose among the people in Alabama; and, though spreading to the rest of the state, the storm center was always in the north.

Of course there had been political differences from the very first, but these agitated the office seekers rather than the settlers. It is very significant for later developments that William H. Crawford, then Secretary of the Treasury under Monroe, controlled by federal patronage in Alabama during the first years of statehood. Tait, Walker, and the Bibbs were his principal adherents within the state. The jealousy created by this situation cemented the anti-Crawford leaders into a union against the Georgia clique. It was probably because North Carolina had sent a number of her prominent citizens to Alabama that she furnished the leading antagonists of the Crawford faction.

Israel Pickens stands out as the first to see the possibilities of the situation and to bring forward an issue which would transform personal differences into real party issues. Provision had been made in the constitution for the establishment of a state bank and an attempt had been made to found such an institution by private subscription, but the necessary capital was not forthcoming and the plan failed. When Pickens came into office, there was pending a scheme for entrusting the fate of the state corporation to the care of the existing private banks, but Pickens vetoed the bill and proposed a bank the capital of which should consist entirely of state funds. The people needed money, and this was to be a people's bank. Though it was not until the beginning of his second term of office that he was able to put the scheme through, the bank, which was founded upon democratic rather than upon financial principles, finally went into operation in 1824 to the great delight of all those who had everything to gain and nothing to lose by the experiment.

By this stroke, Pickens had united the anti-Crawford leaders with the men of the small farmer class, as opposed to the Crawford men from Georgia and the conservative planters and merchants.

In the face of such a combination, the Crawford men had no chance at all and after William Wyatt Bibb and John W. Walker died practically all the more desirable offices were wrested from them. The Georgia men had never been strong in general elections, but in the legislature their power had been great, and even now their partisans were able to make a strong fight in that body.

This situation brings out an important point in Alabama politics. The constitution of 1819 is one of the few original frames of state government which lasted without substantial changes until the War Between the States. This stability was due, in part at least, to the combination of conservatism and progressiveness in the charter which the conditions surrounding its origin promoted. In 1819, Alabama had a large number of poor settlers and a small number of wealthy planters and speculators. The former class had little interest in politics as such, while the latter had many reasons for such an interest. As a matter of course the men who had the time, the ambition, the ability, and the means to engage in politics were chosen to the convention. Thus the unsuspecting settler sent to represent him a man whose point of view was entirely different from his own. Knowing that they could not afford to antagonize the poorer men who greatly outnumbered them, yet wishing to keep the management of the government in their own hands, the framers of the constitution drew up an instrument which was admirably suited to their purposes. While granting manhood suffrage and apportioning representation according to white population, it gave almost supreme authority to the legislature, which in the natural course of events would be largely composed of men of some property.

This arrangement would not have worked as intended had the poorer men ever united to support candidates from among themselves, but this they never did. They accepted their wealthier neighbors as leaders and secured legislation in their favor only when an ambitious politician, such as Pickens, sought popular support through popular measures.

The lack of consistency in the votes of the legislature proclaims an absence of fixed partisan principles and a preponderance of personal vagaries, but when the people voted, they spoke clearly, and two convictions stand out to show the bent of their minds: there was a strong antagonism within the state between north and south, and there was a decided preference for Jackson on the part of the plain men. The conservative class showed a strong prejudice against Jackson, but in 1824 they were outvoted in almost every county in Alabama.

It is significant that both sections of the state were carried for Jackson in 1824. It is also significant that the strongest opposition to him came from the southern cotton-producing area. The percentage of slaves, and hence the strength of the planting interest, was practically the same in the Tennessee Valley as in the Alabama-Tombigbee region. The stronger vote which Jackson received in the former section was due, it would seem, to the greater contrast which existed there between wealth and poverty, and to the class antagonism which the situation engendered. Class antagonism was aggravated by the fact that, though Tennesseeans greatly predominated in the population of the Valley, the planters were largely from other states.

Before the election of 1824, it was generally expected that Adams would carry the southern cotton section of Alabama. The press was strongly in his favor, and the Warrior-Tombigbee section showed a consistent opposition to Jackson in the legislature. The General's unexpected strength here may reasonably be taken to indicate the predominance, even in the heart of the cotton belt, of the men whose votes spoke more powerfully than their arguments—the small farmers.

Because the prairie country was the only extensive region where a large proportion of the soil was suitable for cotton culture, it was only here that the percentage of slaves increased markedly after the first period of settlement was over. Farmers mingled with the planters in all sections of the state, and it is doubtful whether the planters, as a class, could ever have carried more than a few counties of the Black Belt, if they could have done that well. Their success depended upon their ability to draw support from among their neighbors, and the alliance of the anti-Crawford leaders with the farmers on the bank question shows that there was no aversion to such co-operation.

In the matter of the presidency, it seems that the farmers and the planters were very clearly divided on the question of Jacksonism, but in 1828 the desire to defeat Adams was strong enough to unite both classes in support of the General. His old enemies went over with reservations, and their support was only temporary.

Though the Crawford faction had been discredited and the opposition to Jackson had completely lost its hold by 1828, a movement was already under way which was fraught with significance for the future, and which was to put a new face upon the political situation.

The belief in a strict construction of the Constitution is as old as the government, but when Jefferson and his party obtained control, agitation of the point no longer seemed necessary. Possession of power, however, soon changed the point of view of the Republicans, and when the South and the West combined to bring about the War of 1812, the old views seem to have lost much of their weight with Madison and the slave states. It was during this period of Republican supremacy that John Randolph came forward as the champion of state rights, declaring that his party had forsaken its original principles. Henry Adams says that it was Randolph who forecast the policy of Calhoun by uniting the slave interest with the advocacy of strict construction.[1]

It was not until the free states outstripped the slave states in growth and political power that the South as a whole came to realize that its only hope lay in decentralization. But Randolph looked before him and shaped his policy to the future. There were others who shared his views, among them Nathaniel Macon and John Taylor. The connection between these prominent men and the Crawford party of Georgia was close. In a letter to Bolling Hall, Macon maintained the position that to give Congress the right to make internal improvements would be to give it the right to free every slave in the United States.[2]

Under these circumstances, it was not strange that Dixon H. Lewis, the nephew of Bolling Hall, was the first advocate of state rights in Alabama, but the movement was not isolated. The election of John Quincy Adams and the enactment of the tariff of 1824 gave the signal for the revival of anti-nationalistic propaganda in the South. South Carolina, under the influence of William Smith and Thomas Cooper, took the lead in this movement, while in Congress William Giles and John Randolph attacked the administration from the strict constructionist point of view. Calhoun did not come out as leader of the state rights movement until after 1828.[3]

Though the Alabama papers took sides with Giles and Randolph or with Adams, depending on whether they were administration or anti-administration publications, no state except Georgia seems to have influenced Alabama politics directly.

Leaders from the Carolinas and Virginia did not form individual groups but worked in combinations, while those from Georgia formed a distinct faction and thus gave their state a political status in Alabama. Yet, after the fall of the Crawford party, there was not much sympathy between the two commonwealths. The quarrel between Governor Troup and President Adams over the question of removal of the Creek Indians from Georgia excited little friendly interest, most of the local editors taking a critical attitude toward the fiery governor. But in Montgomery County a meeting was held in November, 1826, and here Troup's policy was upheld by some of the leading men of the community.[4] It is natural that such a feeling should have been manifest in this locality, for it was here that the influence of planters from Georgia was strongest. It is also natural that it should have been this county which sent Dixon Hall Lewis to the legislature.

The political ideas of this young man had been shaped by his uncle, Bolling Hall, who was so closely connected with the Crawford faction. Lewis had worked for Crawford in the election of 1824, and now in 1826 he went to Cahawba as a representative in the legislature. His course in opposition to internal improvements and a liberal interpretation of the Constitution was a reflection of a general movement throughout the South. His attitude toward the Troup controversy, and his advocacy of a policy extending the jurisdiction of the state over the Creeks. show his sympathy with the position of the Georgia governor, while his attack upon the state bank exhibits his connection with the old Crawford faction.

The majority of men in Alabama at this time was strongly opposed to the Crawford group, strongly in favor of the state bank, and strongly nationalistic. Yet, by astute political management, Lewis succeeded in gaining some ground for his ideas. The important point is, however, that this scion of the Crawford party was the first leader in Alabama to advocate state rights, and thus he revived a faction which seemed politically dead by making it the bulwark of the slave power through the policy of strict construction.

The significance of this movement was not to become evident until Jackson's attitude toward South Carolina in the nullification controversy raised enemies from among his friends. Then Lewis and the men who believed as he did found their numbers greatly strengthened. When the Whig Party grew up in the South and advocated state rights it became the mouthpiece of the slaveholders. Thus it was Lewis who formed the transition link between the Crawford faction of 1824 and the Whig Party of 1840.

While the slaveholding counties usually came to the support of the Whigs, those where the small farmer predominated usually remained Democratic. Yet it must be remembered that the slave question never entered directly into partisan divisions. If the farmers had united against slavery, they could still have carried practically the entire state, as they did in 1824; for, even in the strongest slaveholding counties, the planters alone could rarely have commanded a majority of the votes. Their success depended upon their ability to carry their farming neighbors with them, which fact is attested to by the great fluctuation in the Whig vote from one campaign to the next.

Other factors, too, are necessary in order to understand the relations between the two parties. The solidly Democratic vote of northern Alabama, despite the large number of slaves in the Tennessee Valley, indicates that the rivalry between the two sections of the state had much to do with political alignments. The sectional votes in other states show that local conditions influenced the result, and that slaveholding was not the only important determining factor. For instance, eastern Tennessee and western North Carolina had a much smaller percentage of slaves than did the Tennessee Valley of Alabama, yet the former sections showed a strong Whig tendency, while the latter was uniformly Democratic.[5]

Thus the eastern part of the Mississippi Territory, with its sparse, isolated settlements, had become the state of Alabama, and within a few decades had a distinct individuality, a thriving trade, and definite political alignments. Seldom in history has an area been settled and developed so rapidly. In 1800 Washington, the eastern county of the Mississippi Territory, included the settlements around St. Stephens and Fort Stoddert which became the nucleus of the State of Alabama. By 1810 Washington and the other two counties of the new state—Baldwin and Madison—had a population of 9,046, including 2,565 slaves. Ten years later Alabama had a population of 144,317.[6] In one decade its population had multiplied sixteen times! The freshness of the wilderness was invigorating, and within the same period the simple cabins were transformed into white pillared mansions, each plantation being a little kingdom in itself. The hunter and the herdsman were no longer in evidence; the slaveowning planter was now the pioneer. This amazing transformation was due partly to the fact that the second-rate did not crawl into power in this new jurisdiction. Men of character and ability were its leaders. The white man, the black man, the red man all had a vital role in this unparalleled development, and each earned a place in the annals of Alabama.[7]

Notes

CHAPTER 1

1. U.S. *Statutes at Large*, II, 229-235.
2. *Ibid.*, II, 455-456.
3. *American State Papers, Lands*, V, 384-385.
4. U.S. *Statutes at Large*, II, 445-446.
5. A. J. Pickett, *History of Alabama*, chap. XXXI.
6. U.S. *Statutes at Large*, II, 229-235.
7. Edmund C. Burnett, contributor, "Papers Relating to Bourbon County, Georgia, 1785-1786," *American Historical Review*, XV (Part I, Oct. 1909; Part 2, Jan. 1910), 66-111, 297-353.
8. *American State Papers, Misc.*, II, 417.
9. E. C. Betts, *Early History of Huntsville, Alabama*, 23-24.
10. Pickett, *Alabama*, 326.
11. Jedidiah Morse, *Report on Indian Affairs*, 167.
12. Benjamin Hawkins, *A Sketch of the Creek Country*, 1798-1799, 44, 45.
13. Pickett, *Alabama*, 469-470.
14. Theodore H. Jack, *Sectionalism and Party Politics in Alabama*, 7.
15. Pickett, *Alabama*, 506.
16. *Ibid.*, 466-469.
17. U.S. *Statutes at Large*, II, 397.
18. R. J. Meigs to George Graham, May 6, 1817, Indian Office files.
19. Good accounts are given in Hawkins, *Creek Country*, 34, 35 *et seq.*; and Morse, *Indian Affairs*, 167 *et seq.*
20. R. J. Meigs to Secretary of War, Nov. 4, 1816 and Silas Dinsmore to John McKee, Oct. 28, 1815, Indian Office files.
21. Bureau of American Ethnology, *Nineteenth Annual Report*, Part I, 104-113.

22. *Southern Advocate*, Apr. 21, 1826.

23. John Bach McMaster, *History of the People of the United States*, 8 vols. (New York, 1883-1913), III, 535-536.

24. Henry Adams, *History of the United States of America*, 9 vols. (New York, 1921), VII, 228-229.

25. McMaster, IX, 162-170; J. S. Bassett, *The Life of Andrew Jackson* (New York, 1928), I, 91-92, 116-117; *Kentucky Gazette*, June 13, 1814.

26. Charles C. Jones, Jr., *The Dead Towns of Georgia* (Collections of the Georgia Historical Society, No. IV [Savannah, 1878]), 234-238.

27. Betts, 22-24.

28. *American State Papers, Misc.*, II, 417.

29. R. J. Meigs to Andrew Jackson, Jan. 17, 1816, Indian Office files; E. P. Gaines to Jackson, Mar. 6, 1817, Andrew Jackson Papers, Library of Congress. There are Jackson MSS in various repositories.

30. Gen. E. P. Gaines to Judge Harry Toulmin, June 1, 1815, and Judge Toulmin to Gov. David Holmes, June 5, 1815, Toulmin-Holmes Correspondence.

31. *Washington Republican*, Oct. 21, 1815.

32. Gov. David Holmes, Proclamation of June 29, 1815, Executive Journal, 1814-1817.

33. *Washington Republican*, Jan. 10, 1816; William H. Crawford to Jackson, Jan. 27, 1816, Jackson Papers.

34. *Ibid.*, June 12, 1816.

35. See Bureau of American Ethnology, *Eighteenth Annual Report*, Plate I.

36. Gov. David Holmes, Proclamation of May 9, 1817, Executive Journal.

CHAPTER 2

1. The description given here is based almost entirely upon that by Roland M. Harper in "A Preliminary Soil Census of Alabama and West Florida," and in his *Economic Botany of Alabama*, though the writer has relied to some extent upon his personal knowledge of the country.

2. In addition to the map given here, see that by Eugene A. Smith, *U.S. Census, 1880*, VI, 9; and that in U.S. Dept. of Agriculture, *Atlas of American Agriculture*, Cotton Section (Washington, D.C., 1936), 8.

3. See H. F. Cleland, "The Black Belt of Alabama," *Geographical Review*, X, 375-387.

4. Letter from Dr. J. W. Heustis of Cahawba, Apr. 1, 1821, in the *Cahawba Press and Alabama State Intelligencer*, June 2, 1821.

5. Based upon maps made from the tract books in the office of the Secretary of State, Montgomery, Ala.; Weymouth T. Jordan, *Ante-Bellum Alabama, Town and Country* (Florida State Univ. Stud., No. 27 [Tallahassee, 1957]), 22-25.

6. See R. M. Harper in *South Atlantic Quarterly*, XIX, 201.

CHAPTER 3

1. *Atlas of American Agriculture*, Cotton Section, 16, 18.

2. U. B. Phillips, *A History of Transportation in the Eastern Cotton Belt to 1860*, 46-56.

3. *Atlas of American Agriculture*, Cotton Section, 18.

4. *American State Papers*, Misc., II, 417.

5. *Ibid.*, Lands, V, 384-385; T. P. Abernethy, *The South in the New Nation*, chap. XVI.

6. This statement is strongly supported by the cases where the writer has been able to ascertain the origin of the immigrants.

7. A. Hodgson, *Letters from North America*, I, 138; *Savannah Republican*, Feb. 25, Mar. 8, 1818; see Abernethy, "The Great Migration," *The South in the New Nation*.

8. John D. Bibb, *Sketch of William Bibb*, A. J. Pickett Papers.

9. R. J. Meigs to Louis Winston, June 12, 1815, Indian Office files.

10. Instructions from William H. Crawford, Jan. 27, 1816, Jackson Papers; Jackson to William H. Crawford, July 4, 1816, and R. J. Meigs to Louis Winston, June 12, 1815, Indian Office files.

11. An interesting letter from Clabon Harris to General Jackson, Fort Claiborne, Jan. 12, 1816, gives an account of the conditions of some of the squatters. See Jackson Papers.

12. A. B. Meek MS., "Early Settlement of Alabama."

13. Cherokee Chiefs to R. J. Meigs, Mar. 20, 1817, and Samuel Riley to R. J. Meigs, Indian Office files; E. P. Gaines to Jackson, Mar. 6, 1817, Jackson Papers.

14. The map given here is based upon that prepared by John Melish for 1818, but it has been compared with all those in the Library of Congress for the period covered. Information as to principal routes of communication is based also upon accounts of travel available to the writer.

15. It seems that this road was not actually opened until 1811. See Phillips, *Transportation*, 69, and T. H. Ball, *Clarke County and Its Surroundings*, 134.

16. Phillips, *Transportation*, 68-69.

17. Betts, 21.

18. Land Office, *Record of Proclamations*, May, 24, 1807.

19. The account given here of the distribution of population in Alabama agrees, in general, with the available statements concerning different localities and with the general statements to be found in William Garrett, *Reminiscences of Public Men in Alabama for Thirty Years*, 35; Meek MS., "Early Settlement of Alabama." See also P. J. Hamilton, *Colonial Mobile*, 1519-1821, 456-457 and Nelson F. Smith, *History of Pickens County*, 37-39.

20. Phillips, *Transportation*, 63.

21. Meek MS., "Early Settlement of Alabama" and George Powell, *History of Blount County*, 37.

22. V. Gayle Snedecor, *A Directory of Greene County for 1855-6*.

23. Extract of a letter to the editor of the *Newburyport* (Mass.) *Herald*, dated Claiborne (A), March, 1823; *Alabama Republican*, Aug. 15, 1823; Col. Will King to Jackson, Nov. 23, 1821, Jackson Papers.

24. M. P. Blue MS., I, "Autauga County," 4; Albert Burton Moore, *History of Alabama and Her People*, 72-74.

CHAPTER 4

1. *Annals of Congress*, 8 Cong., 1 Sess., 624.

2. *Ibid.*, 11 Cong., Pt. 1, 695; Abernethy, 455-456, 473-474.

3. McMaster, III, 371 *et seq*.

4. *American State Papers*, Misc., II, 155; Clarence E. Carter (ed.), *The Territory of Alabama (The Territorial Papers of the United States)*, XVIII, 279, 293.

5. *American State Papers*, Misc., II, 163-164.

6. J. W. Walker to George Poindexter, Dec. 23, 1812, Mississippi Transcripts.

7. J. F. H. Claiborne, *Mississippi as a Province, Territory, and State*, 350; Cowles Mead to George Poindexter, Dec. 23, 1812, Mississippi Transcripts.

8. Payson Jackson Treat, *The National Land System, 1785-1820* (New York, 1910), 355-364.

9. *Washington Republican*, Sept. 9, 1815, Mar. 13 and Apr. 17, 1816, Apr. 9, 1817.

10. *American State Papers, Misc.*, II, 182.

11. *Annals of Congress*, 12 Cong., 1 Sess., II, 1480.

12. *Washington Republican*, Apr. 5 and 26, 1815.

13. *Annals of Congress*, 14 Cong., 1 Sess., 352; *Washington Republican*, Apr. 16, 1817.

14. *Ibid.*, May 22 and 29, 1816.

15. *Ibid.*, Nov. 13, 1816; James Titus to Jackson, Dec. 5, 1816, Jackson Papers.

16. William Darby, *Emigrant's Guide*, 107-113; *Washington Republican*, Jan. 22, Feb. 26, Mar. 5, 1817.

17. *U.S. Statutes at Large*, III, 490.

18. *Ibid.*, III, 371-372; Carter, XVIII, 53-57.

19. Alma C. Tompkins, *Charles Tait*, 12-16; J. W. Walker to C. Tait, Jan. 18, 1817, Charles A. Tait Papers.

20. A. P. Hayne to Jackson, Nov. 27, 1816, Jackson Papers.

21. Meek MS., "The Alabama Territory."

22. Pickett, *Alabama*, 615; John Monette, *History of the Valley of the Mississippi*, 446-447.

23. Pickett, *Alabama*, 615-617.

24. Jesse S. Reeves, *The Napoleonic Exiles in America*, 525-656; Thomas W. Martin, *French Military Adventurers in Alabama, 1818-1828, passim.*

CHAPTER 5

1. J. W. Walker to C. Tait, Nov. 11, 1818, Tait Papers.

2. J. W. Walker to C. Tait, Nov. 9 and 15, 1818, *ibid.*

3. W. W. Bibb to C. Tait, Sept. 19, 1818, *ibid.*

4. J. W. Walker to C. Tait, Nov. (?), 1818, *ibid.*

5. J. W. Walker to C. Tait, Feb. 8, 1819, *ibid.*

6. *Alabama Republican*, Feb. 6, 1819. The editor states that Crowell said that he remonstrated before a congressional committee in regard to the admission of Alabama, and that this remonstrance was probably against the rule of representation for the Constitutional Convention as adopted by the Alabama Legislature.

7. *U.S. Statutes at Large*, III, 489-492.

8. Tompkins, 12-16; J. W. Walker to C. Tait, Jan. 18, 1817, Tait Papers.

9. William H. Thomas, "The Birth and Growth of the Constitution of Alabama," 4-5.

10. *Journal of the Constitutional Convention of 1819.*

11. *Constitution of the State of Alabama, 1819.*

12. *Ibid.*, Schedule, sec. 7.

13. W. W. Bibb to C. Tait, Sept. 19, 1818, Tait Papers.

14. *Journal of the House of Representatives of the State of Alabama, 1819-1828*, 37.

15. J. W. Walker to C. Tait, Aug. 7, 1819, Tait Papers; *Dictionary of American Biography*, X, 406-407.

16. Pickett, *Alabama*, 641-647.

17. W. H. Crawford to C. Tait, Nov. 7, 1819, Tait Papers.

18. H. Toulmin to J. W. Walker, Feb. 21, 1819, John Williams Walker Papers.

19. C. Tait to J. W. Walker, Nov. 19, 1819, *ibid.*

20. W. H. Crawford to C. Tait, Nov. 29, 1819, Tait Papers.

21. J. W. Walker to C. Tait, Dec. 20, 1819, *ibid.*

22. C. Tait to J. W. Walker, Oct. 9, 1819, Walker Papers; W. H. Crawford to C. Tait, Nov. 7 and 29, 1819, Tait Papers.

23. Pickett, *Alabama*, 661-662.

24. *House Journal, 1819*, 45.

25. William Birney, *James G. Birney and his Times*, 40.

26. W. W. Bibb to C. Tait, Sept. 19, 1818, Tait Papers.

27. J. W. Walker to C. Tait, Jan. 19, 1819, *ibid.*

28. W. H. Crawford to Gov. Holmes, Apr. 22, 1818, Mississippi Transcripts.

29. J. C. Calhoun to C. Tait, Sept. 5, 1818, Tait Papers.

CHAPTER 6

1. *Atlas of American Agriculture*, Cotton Section, 20.

2. D. R. Dewey, *Financial History of the United States*, 151.

3. *Ibid.*, 153.

4. *Annals of Congress*, 16 Cong., 2 Sess., 233.

5. *U.S. Statutes at Large*, III, 116-117.

6. Treat, 111-112, 120-121.

7. Thomas Freeman to Jackson, Apr. 12, 1816, Jackson Papers.

8. A. P. Hayne to Jackson, Nov. 27, 1816, *ibid.*

9. D. Parker to Jackson, Jan. 6, 1817, *ibid.*

10. A. P. Hayne to Jackson, Nov. 27, 1816, *ibid.*

11. Land Office, *Record of Proclamations*, May 24, 1817.

12. A. P. Hayne to Jackson, Aug. 5, 1817, Jackson Papers.

13. *American State Papers, Lands*, V, 384-385.

14. Tract Book of Montgomery County, Office of the Secretary of State, Montgomery, Ala.

15. A. P. Hayne to Jackson, Aug. 5, 1817, Jackson Papers.

16. Meek MS., "Early Settlement of Alabama," 1815-1819.

17. Land Office, *Record of Proclamations*, Nov. 1, 1817, and Mar. 31, 1818.

18. *American State Papers, Lands*, V, 384-385.

19. John Coffee to Jackson, Feb. 12, 1818, Jackson-Coffee MS.

20. Record of Deeds, Dallas County, D, 305.

21. *Niles' Weekly Register*, XVI, 192; *Halcyon and Tombeckbee Public Advertiser* (hereafter *St. Stephens Halcyon*) Oct. 11, 1819; *Alabama Republican*, May 1, 1818.

22. *American State Papers, Lands*, V, 378-380, 513.

23. *Ibid.*, 645.

24. *U.S. Statutes at Large*, III, 566.

25. *Ibid.*, III, 612-614.

26. *American State Papers, Lands*, IV, 795.

27. *Ibid., Lands*, V, 513, 800.

28. *Southern Advocate*, May 19, 1826.

29. Nelson F. Smith, *History of Pickens County, Alabama*, 42-44; *Cahawba Press*, Oct. 29, 1821.

30. B. F. Riley, *History of Conecuh County, Alabama*, 96.

31. *House Journal*, 1825, 96-97; *American State Papers, Lands*, IV, 529; *ibid.*, V, 380-382; *Southern Advocate*, Apr. 28, June 23, Sept. 29, Oct. 6, 1826.

32. *U.S. Statutes at Large*, IV, 158-159.

CHAPTER 7

1. In addition to the U.S. Census of 1820 and 1830, that taken by the Mississippi Territory in 1816 (*American State Papers, Misc.*, II, 408); the census of Alabama Territory taken in 1818 (Walker Papers); and those taken by the State of Alabama in 1824 (Huntsville *Democrat*, Nov. 22, 1824 and Dec. 14, 1827) are extant.

2. This view is based partly on charts made from the tract books of Clarke, Montgomery, Dallas, and Perry counties.

3. Pickett, *Alabama*, 325.

4. *Ibid.*, 503.

5. Justus Wyman, "A Geographical Sketch of the Alabama Territory" in *Alabama Historical Society Transactions*, III, 126.

6. Darby, 33.

7. See Pickett's *Alabama*, chap. XLV.

8. *Southern Advocate*, July 1, 1825; *Alabama Journal*, Sept. 15, 1826; *Mobile Commercial Register*, Dec. 1, 1827, Jan. 8, Apr. 15,

May 17, Oct. 8, 1828; *Southern Agriculturist* (from the *Alabama Journal*), I, 379.

9. See Phillips, *American Negro Slavery*, chap. X, for an account of the westward movement of the cotton planter.

10. A. Hodgson, *Letters*, I, 39.

11. Duke Bernhard of Saxe-Weimar, *Travels Through North America During the Years 1825 and 1826*, I, 30-31.

12. This is the writer's interpretation of the facts, but the general idea is completely borne out by the following passage from James Stuart's *Three Years in North America*, II, 160: "The planters' houses in the southern states are very different in their mode of construction from those in the north. The common form of the planters' houses, and indeed of all houses that you meet with on the roadside in this country, is two square pens, with an open space between them, connected by a roof above and a floor below, so as to form a parallelogram of nearly triple the length of its depth. In the open space the family take their meals during very good weather. The kitchen and the places for slaves are all separate buildings, as are the stable, cow-barns, etc. About ten buildings of this description make up the establishment of an ordinary planter, with half a dozen slaves."

13. *Alabama Republican*, Nov. 14, 1823; *Cahawba Press*, Dec. 20, 1823, Jan. 7, 1826; *St. Stephens Halcyon*, May 1, 1820.

14. *Alabama Republican*, Aug. 25, 1820.

15. Wyman, 126; *American Farmer*, III, 299; A. P. Hayne to Jackson, Aug. 6, 1820, Jackson Papers.

16. Phillips, *Slavery*, chap. XV.

17. *American Farmer*, IV, 308-309. See also Phillips, *Slavery*, chap. XV.

18. C. Tait to J. W. Walker, Nov. 19, 1819, Walker Papers.

19. A. Hodgson, *Letters*, I, 206-207.

20. *American Farmer*, VIII, 222-223, quoting a letter from John Pope of Florence, Ala., dated Sept. 29, 1826; *Southern Agriculturist*, II, 255; M. B. Hammond, *The Cotton Industry*, 76-77; Thomas G. Fessenden, *The Complete Farmer*, 263-265.

21. Anne Royall, *Letters from Alabama on Various Subjects, 1817-1822*, 62.

22. An excellent description of the method of preparing cotton for market was furnished the *Nashville Agriculturist* by Alexander McDonald of Eufaula, Ala., in 1845. It is reprinted in *Senate Documents*, 1 Sess., 29 Cong., VI, No. 307. Though this is later than the period under discussion, it gives a clear idea of the problems and methods of ginning and baling cotton on a plantation.

23. *Alabama Republican*, Feb. 15 and Mar. 22, 1822.

24. *Mobile Register*, Mar. 26, 1824.

25. *Cahawba Press*, Jan. 21, 1822; *American Farmer*, IV, 380-382.

26. *Alabama Republican*, Sept. 7, and Nov. 23, 1821, Sept. 27, 1822; *Cahawba Press*, Dec. 13, 1821, Jan. 28, 1822.

27. Saxe-Weimar, I, 33; *Southern Advocate*, July 21, 1826; *Southern Agriculturist*, II, 254-262; Royall, *Letters* (quoting letter from Col. Pope), 162.

28. *American Farmer*, II, 116; *Southern Advocate*, Sept. 8 and 29, 1826; Huntsville *Democrat*, Sept. 8, 1826.

29. *Southern Advocate*, Nov. 17, 1826.

30. For yearly average of prices for middling upland cotton in New York and Liverpool, see J. L. Watkins, *Production and Price of Cotton for a Hundred Years*, 8-9.

31. For chart of slave prices, see Phillips, *Slavery*, 370.

32. *Alabama Republican*, Nov. 2, 1821.

33. *Mobile Argus*, Oct. 31, 1823; Huntsville *Democrat*, Oct. 28, 1823; *Alabama Republican*, Oct. 24, 1823.

34. Samuel Hazard, *U.S. Commercial and Statistical Register* (Philadelphia, 1840-42), III, 272.

35. *Tuscumbian*, June 27, 1825.

36. *Alabama Journal*, Sept. 29, 1826; *Southern Advocate*, Sept. 15, 1826, Dec. 1, 1827; Huntsville *Democrat*, Mar. 9, 1827.

37. *Journal of the Senate of Alabama, 1819-1828* (hereafter *Senate Journal*), 1826, 9.

38. Statistics for Madison County for 1819 give 825 pounds as the average for a full hand. See *Alabama Republican*, Aug. 25, 1820. James G. Birney is said to have produced 1,850 pounds to the hand in 1820. See James Jackson to Andrew Jackson, May 28, 1821, Jackson Papers. But a thousand pounds to the hand is mentioned in most estimates as the average.

39. A. Hodgson, *Letters*, I, 124; Riley, *Conecuh County*, 52; *Southern Advocate*, Sept. 7, 1827.

40. *Jefferson County and Birmingham*, 59; Riley, *Conecuh County*, 22-25, 92-111; Smith, *Pickens County*, 46-48; W. E. W. Yerby, *History of Greensboro, Alabama*, 3; Carter, V, 724-725, 743.

41. Based on statements published in the *Southern Advocate*, Dec. 1, 1826.

42. See Chapter 9.

43. "Documentary History of Industrial Society" from the *Georgia Courier*, Oct. 11, 1827, 283-298.

44. *Mobile Register*, Jan. 6, 1823.

45. *Alabama Republican,* Mar. 1, 1822; Huntsville *Democrat,* Jan. 19, 1827; Jordan, 34-36.

46. W. G. Robertson, *Recollections of the Early Settlers of Montgomery County,* 11-13, 15-16, 36-38, 125, 139-140.

47. *Mobile Register,* Mar. 2, 1824.

48. Riley, *Conecuh County,* 19, 28-32, 43-54, 55-65.

49. See Frank L. Owsley, *Plain Folk of the Old South* (Baton Rouge, 1949).

CHAPTER 8

1. *Niles' Register,* XXII, 96; *Mobile Register,* Feb. 7, 1822.

2. A. Hodgson, *Letters,* I, 152.

3. Saxe-Weimar, I, 39-41; P. J. Hamilton, *Colonial Mobile, 1519-1821,* 473; *Mobile Argus,* Oct. 28, 1823; *Mobile Advertiser,* Feb. 26, 1824.

4. *St. Stephens Halcyon,* Mar. 30, 1822.

5. *Alabama Republican,* May 4, 1821; Hamilton, *Colonial Mobile,* 463.

6. Thomas S. Woodward, *Reminiscences of the Creek or Muscogee Indians,* 130; M. P. Blue, *History of Montgomery,* 6-8. See Pickett, *Alabama,* 592. Pickett states that the County of Montgomery was named for Major Lemuel Montgomery, who was first to fall on the breastworks at Horseshoe Bend, but that the town was named "in memory of his relation who fell at Quebec."

7. Saxe-Weimar, I, 35.

8. A. Levasseur, *Lafayette en Amerique en 1824 et 1825,* II, 345; *Niles' Register,* XXI, 215; E. P. Gaines to Jackson, Mar. 15, 1816, Jackson Papers. See Phillips, *Transportation,* 71, for a description of the flat-bottomed and pole boats.

9. Hines Holt to B. Hall, July 4, Sept. 20, and Nov. 14, 1820, Hall Papers.

10. *Niles' Register,* XX, 63, *House Executive Documents,* No. 15, 20 Cong., 2 Sess., Vol. 1.

11. *Alabama Republican,* Feb. 8, 1822.

12. Betts, 61-62; *Alabama Republican,* Jan. 18, 1822.

13. *Washington Republican,* Jan. 1, 1817; D. B. Warden, *A Statistical, Political, and Historical Account of the United States of North America,* III, 39; S. D. Hutchings to R. J. Meigs, Dec. 3, 1816, Indian Office files.

14. *Alabama Republican,* Jan. 18, 1822.

15. Jedidiah Morse, *Universal Geography,* I, 558.

16. Hamilton, *Colonial Mobile*, 447-448, 471-472.

17. *Mobile Gazette*, Aug. 4, 1819, copied in the *Alabama Republican*, Aug. 21, 1819.

18. *Ibid.*, Apr. 3, 1819.

19. *St. Stephens Halcyon*, May 15, 1820.

20. Hamilton, *Colonial Mobile*, 172; J. S. Walker to J. W. Walker, Nov. 23, 1821, Walker Papers. In 1822, the *Elizabeth*, the *Harriett*, the *Cotton Plant*, and the *Tensa* were navigating the Alabama, while the *Tombeckbee* was plying the Tombigbee River. *Mobile Register*, June 10, 1822.

21. *Cahawba Press*, Apr. 24, 1824.

22. Statistics on the trade for the seasons 1826-1827 and 1827-1828 collected from the *Mobile Register*.

23. *Mobile Argus*, Oct. 28, 1823.

24. *Mobile Register*, Dec. 19, 1826.

25. Saxe-Weimar, I, 32-38.

26. *Alabama Republican*, Mar. 16, 1821.

27. *Ibid.*, Jan. 18 and Mar. 15, 1822.

28. *Ibid.*, May 17, 1822; *Tuscumbian*, Aug. 22, 1825, May 8, 1826.

29. *Alabama Republican*, Jan. 18, 1822; *Southern Advocate*, Mar. 14, 1828.

30. *Ibid.*, Feb. 15 and Mar. 14, 1828.

31. *Acts of the General Assembly of Alabama*, 1819-1828 (hereafter *Alabama Acts*), 1823, 66-69; *ibid.*, 1828, 79-86; *Southern Advocate*, Mar. 2, 1827.

32. *American State Papers, Military*, II, 698-701.

33. *Ibid., Military*, IV, 13; Huntsville *Democrat*, July 11, 1828.

34. *U.S. Statutes at Large*, IV, 290.

35. *Alabama Acts*, 1823, 62-66.

36. *House Executive Documents*, No. 15, 20 Cong., 2 Sess., Vol. I.

37. *House Reports*, No. 48, 20 Cong., 1 Sess., I, 176.

38. A. Hodgson, *Letters*, I, 273.

39. *U.S. Statutes at Large*, III, 315; *American State Papers, Military*, IV, 627.

40. *Ibid., Misc.*, II, 537; *Alabama Republican*, Dec. 17, 1819, June 9, 1820; William H. Crawford to Jackson, Mar. 8, 1816 and W. Young to Jackson, Mar. 14, 1817, Jackson Papers.

41. *American State Papers, Post Office Dept.*, 119-120; *Tuscumbian*, Nov. 12, 1824.

42. *Alabama Republican*, May 6, 1820.

43. *Ibid.*, Aug. 16 and Sept. 13, 1822.

44. *Tuscumbian*, Apr. 11, 1825.

45. *American State Papers, Post Office Dept.*, 241; *Southern Advocate*, Sept. 4, 1827.

46. *House Reports*, No. 48, 20 Cong., 1 Sess., 176.

47. Blue, *History of Montgomery*, 11-12; *Alabama Journal*, June 23 and 30, 1826.

48. *Mobile Register*, Nov. 24, 1827.

49. *American State Papers, Military*, III, 137-138.

50. *House Executive Documents*, No. 156, 19 Cong., 1 Sess., Vol. IX; *House Reports*, No. 48, 20 Cong., 1 Sess., 1; *American State Papers, Military*, III, 109; Huntsville *Democrat*, Sept. 7, 1827.

51. *House Executive Documents*, No. 125, 20 Cong., 1 Sess., Vol. III; letter from Gabriel Moore in the *Southern Advocate*, Jan. 13, 1826.

52. Pickett, *Alabama*, 466-479.

53. O. D. Street, *Marshall County One Hundred Years Ago*, 8.

54. Warden, III, 39.

55. *Alabama Republican*, Mar. 1, 1822.

CHAPTER 9

1. Riley, *Conecuh County*, 22-25.

2. See Chapter 6 for a discussion of the Second Bank of the United States.

3. *American State Papers, Finance*, III, 765-766.

4. Advertisement of P. Yeatman & Co. in *Alabama Republican*, Sept. 22, 1820; Oct. 6, 1820, *ibid.*; also statistics on bank note exchange collected from newspapers.

5. Statistics on bank note exchange in Huntsville and Tuscumbia, collected from newspapers.

6. *Mobile Register*, Oct. 5, 1824. Exports for the year 1824 included 14,990 bales of cotton to New York, 13,094 to New Orleans, and 8,778 to Liverpool.

7. *Mobile Register*, Nov. 7, 1822; Feb. 17, 1824.

8. John Hunter to Nicholas Biddle, Jan. 6, 1827, Nicholas Biddle Papers.

9. See Alfred H. Stone, "The Cotton Factorage System of the Southern States," *American Historical Review*, XX, 557-565. This system came to be the usual practice, but whether it was completely developed during the 'twenties cannot be stated definitely. Merchants frequently advertised that they would advance on cotton turned over to them for shipment, but a committee of the legisla-

ture estimated in 1826 that two-thirds of the cotton shipped to Mobile was sold by the negotiation of bills of exchange, and the banks of that town did a large business in such paper. The fact that the planters received payments in these bills indicates that the local merchants were hardly more than purchasing agents for their eastern correspondents.

Another indication of sales on a cash basis is the prevalence of auctions in Mobile at this time. It was customary to beat a drum as an announcement of the sale, and the noise made in this way came to be such a nuisance that complaint was made in the newspapers. But country merchants doubtless made advances to small producers in their neighborhood from the very first. See *House Journal*, 1826, 80; *Southern Advocate*, May 12, 1826; *Mobile Register*, Apr. 21, 1823, Jan. 17, 1824.

10. *Journal of the Senate of Alabama, 1819-1828* (hereafter *Senate Journal*), 1819, 188-190.

11. *American State Papers, Finance*, IV, 745.

12. *Mobile Register*, Oct. 29, 1823, Aug. 30, 1828.

13. Horace White, *Money and Banking* (Boston and New York, 1935), 33-34.

14. *Alabama Republican*, Nov. 10, 1820.

15. *Ibid.*, May 18 and June 29, 1821; *Cahawba Press*, June 8, 1822.

16. Statistics on London exchange collected from newspapers; extract from the *National Gazette* in *Alabama Republican*, Feb. 12, 1822.

17. *House Journal*, 1826, 80; *American State Papers, Finance*, III, 762; statistics on domestic exchange collected from newspapers.

18. Message of Gov. Pickens in *Senate Journal*, 1821, 21.

CHAPTER 10

1. Harry Toulmin, A *Digest of the Laws of the State of Alabama* (hereafter *Alabama Code of 1823*).

2. *American State Papers, Finance*, III, 767-768.

3. *Ibid., Finance*, IV, 740.

4. *Ibid., Finance*, III, 778-782.

5. *Ibid., Finance*, III, 764.

6. *Ibid., Finance*, III, 768.

7. *Ibid., Finance*, III, 765-766.

8. *Cahawba Press*, Oct. 15, 1821.

9. *Senate Journal*, 1821, 8-9.

10. Pickett, *Alabama*, 666-668.

11. Huntsville *Democrat*, Dec. 16, 1823.
12. Toulmin, *Alabama Code of 1823*.
13. *Alabama Republican*, June 29, 1821.
14. *Senate Journal*, 1821, 8-9.
15. *House Journal*, 1821, 227.
16. *Cahawba Press*, July 30, 1821.
17. *House Journal*, 1822, 25.
18. *Cahawba Press*, Feb. 4, Apr. 27, and May 25, 1822; *St. Stephens Halcyon*, Feb. 9, 1822.
19. Huntsville *Democrat*, July 20, 1824.
20. *Senate Journal*, 1821, 27-34; *House Journal*, 1822, 9 et seq.
21. *Alabama Republican*, Aug. 24, 1821; *Mobile Argus*, Nov. 6, 1823; *Mobile Advertiser*, Dec. 15, 1823.
22. *Alabama Republican*, Oct. 17, 1823.
23. Huntsville *Democrat*, Oct. 14, 1823; *Alabama Republican*, Dec. 12, 1823.
24. Huntsville *Democrat*, Mar. 30, 1824; *Franklin Enquirer*, Apr. 7, 1824.
25. *Alabama Republican*, June 13, 1823; *Mobile Argus*, July 22, 1823.
26. *Alabama Acts*, Dec. 20, 1823.
27. *Senate Journal*, 1823, 65.
28. *Senate Journal*, 1824, 7.
29. *Ibid.*, 1825, 10; *Alabama Republican*, Feb. 18, 1825.
30. Huntsville *Democrat*, Apr. 27, 1824.
31. *Southern Advocate*, Sept. 8 and 15, 1826.
32. Huntsville *Democrat*, Mar. 9, 1827.
33. *Southern Advocate*, Jan. 5, 1827.
34. *Mobile Register*, Nov. 18, 1826; *Alabama Journal*, May 6, 1826; *Senate Journal*, 1826, 9.
35. *Senate Journal*, 1827, 184-185; Huntsville *Democrat*, Apr. 13, 1827; *Mobile Register*, June 25, 1828.
36. *Alabama Acts*, Jan. 12, 1828.
37. *American State Papers, Lands*, VI, 891; *Southern Advocate*, Feb. 1, 1828.
38. *Senate Journal*, 1828, 18.

CHAPTER 11

1. On the subject of the Georgia parties, see U. B. Phillips, *Georgia and State Rights*, chap. IV.
2. William H. Crawford to C. Tait, Nov. 7, ʒ819, Tait Papers.

3. Letter copied from the *Franklin Gazette* in *Mobile Argus*, Mar. 3, 1823.

4. Jack F. Ross to Bolling Hall, Aug. 25, 1821, Bolling Hall Papers; William H. Crawford to C. Tait, Nov. 27, 1819, Tait Papers.

5. William H. Crawford to C. Tait, Nov. 29, 1819, *ibid.*

6. C. Tait to W. W. Bibb, Nov. 28, 1820, Bibb Papers.

7. *Alabama Republican*, Mar. 25, 1824; Huntsville *Democrat*, Nov. 11, 1823, July 20, 1824.

8. The origin of the population in different sections of the state has been discussed in Chapter 3. The statement of the political tendencies of the various sections is based upon the attitude of the press and the presidential vote of 1824.

9. *Cahawba Press*, Dec. 14, 1822; Huntsville *Democrat*, July 20, Dec. 14 and 21, 1824; *Alabama Republican*, Dec. 17, 1824; William H. Crawford to C. Tait, Feb. 16, 1823, Tait Papers.

10. *Alabama Republican*, May 21 and Oct. 8, 1824; *Cahawba Press*, July 10, 1824; Huntsville *Democrat*, June 24, 1824.

11. *American Mirror*, May 29, 1824. Jackson did not refer simply to munitions of war but meant to include all articles necessary to put the country in a condition of economic independence, considering this necessary to military safety. See letters to John Coffee, dated May 7 and June 18, 1824, in Jackson-Coffee MS.

12. Huntsville *Democrat*, Aug. 24, 1824; *Alabama Republican*, Aug. 8 and Oct. 1, 1824.

13. *Senate Journal*, 1823, 12; *Alabama Republican*, Sept. 26, 1823.

14. *Senate Journal*, 1823, 82; *House Journal*, 1823, 77.

15. *Ibid.*, 1823, 120-125.

16. *Niles' Register*, XXV, 323-324, 362.

17. Greensboro *Halcyon*, Nov. 1, 1823.

18. Pickett, *Alabama*, 653-654.

19. *Cahawba Press*, May 8, 1824.

20. *Ibid.*, June 18, 1824.

21. *Ibid.*, June 28 and July 7, 1824.

22. The returns are to be found in the Huntsville *Democrat* for Nov. 22, 1824, and in the *Cahawba Press* of the same date.

CHAPTER 12

1. Excerpt from the *Nashville Gazette* in the *Tuscumbian*, Mar. 7, 1825.

2. Huntsville *Democrat*, Nov. 7, 1826.

3. *House Journal*, 1825, 75; *Senate Journal*, 1825, 47.

4. J. W. Walker to C. Tait, Sept. 22, 1818, Tait Papers.

5. H. M. Somerville, *Trial of the Alabama Supreme Court Judges in 1829*, 62-75; R. C. Brickel, *Digest of the Decisions of the Supreme Court of the State of Alabama* (hereafter Brickel's *Digest*), II, Pt. 1, 4-5; *Southern Advocate*, Feb. 9 and Mar. 9, 1827; Huntsville *Democrat*, Jan. 19, 1827.

6. *Ibid.*, Feb. 9, 1827.

7. For a sketch of Clay's career, see Pickett, *Alabama*, 648-653.

8. *Southern Advocate*, Jan. 12, 1827; Huntsville *Democrat*, Dec. 29, 1826.

9. *Ibid.*, Oct. 27, 1826.

10. *Senate Journal, 1826*, 20-21.

11. *Ibid., 1826*, 193.

12. *Ibid., 1828*, 76; *Mobile Register*, Nov. 21, 1828.

13. The *Southern Advocate* for Sept. 19, 1828, published toasts drunk at a dinner given the congressional delegation of Alabama. Here the tariff was condemned and internal improvements supported.

14. *Ibid.*, Apr. 25, 1828. Jackson's letter is dated Feb. 28, 1828.

15. *Ibid.*, Oct. 14, 1825, Mar. 16, 1827; Huntsville *Democrat*, July 29 and Sept. 16, 1825; *Tuscumbian*, Nov. 7, 1825.

16. *Senate Journal, 1826*, 11.

17. *Alabama Sessional Acts, 1826*, 32.

18. *Senate Journal, 1826*, 101-102; *ibid., 1828*, 207. In the latter instance there were stricken from a resolution condemning the tariff the following words: "and that open and unqualified resistance should only be the *dernier ressort.*"

19. Huntsville *Democrat*, Nov. 7, 1828.

20. *Southern Advocate*, Nov. 7, 1828.

21. *Mobile Register*, July 12, 1828.

22. Obituary of Dixon Hall Lewis, MS. in William L. Yancey Papers. See also Thomas M. Williams, *Dixon H. Lewis*. There are brief sketches of Lewis in Thomas M. Owen, *History of Alabama and Dictionary of Alabama Biography*, IV, 1043-1044; DAB, XI, 209-210.

23. *Senate Journal, 1826*, 101-102.

24. *House Journal, 1828*, 220, 223.

25. *Ibid., 1828*, 263.

26. *Cahawba Press*, Mar. 18, 1826.

27. Lewis obituary, 15, Yancey Papers; see *House Journal, 1826*, 223-224, for report on finances.

28. *House Journal, 1827*, 182 *et seq.*

29. The Huntsville *Democrat* for Dec. 5, 1828, gives the vote as follows: Jackson, 13,384; Adams, 1,629.

CHAPTER 13

1. Clarence S. Brigham, *History and Bibliography of American Newspapers* (Worcester, Mass., 1947), I, 4.

2. *Ibid.*, I, 5; Betts, 80.

3. *Southern Advocate*, May 6, 1823.

4. *Alabama Republican*, Oct. 10, 1823.

5. A. B. Meek, *Romantic Passages in Southwestern History*, 103-104; Carter, *The Territory of Alabama*, XVIII, 547 fn.

6. Blue, *History of Montgomery*, 12.

7. *Mobile Register*, May 9, 1822.

8. *St. Stephens Halcyon*, Nov. 2, 1822; *Cahawba Press*, Nov. 22, 1822.

9. *Ibid.*, Nov. 29, 1823.

10. Blue, *History of Montgomery*, 12.

11. Blue MS., "Dallas County," 16.

12. *Cahawba Press*, Sept. 25, 1824; *American Mirror*, Sept. 11, 1824.

13. *Senate Journal*, 1823, 96-97; *ibid.*, 1824, 38-39; *ibid.*, 1825, 35.

14. *Cahawba Press*, June 21, 1823.

15. *Alabama Republican*, June 11, 1824.

16. *Tuscumbian*, Apr. 18, 1825.

17. Huntsville *Democrat*, Sept. 15, 1826.

18. *Ibid.*, Aug. 24, 1824.

19. *Ibid.*, Sept. 15, 1826.

20. Isabella Margaret Blandin, *History of Higher Education of Women in the South Prior to 1860* (New York and Washington, 1901), 59.

21. A. Hodgson, *Letters*, I, 144, 269.

22. *Alabama Acts*, Dec. 18, 1819, Jan. 1, 1823.

23. Huntsville *Democrat*, Feb. 9, May 18 and June 29, 1827.

24. *House Journal*, 1826, 244.

25. *U.S. Statutes at Large*, IV, 237.

26. *Alabama Acts*, Jan. 15, 1828.

27. Toulmin, *Alabama Code of 1823*.

28. *Alabama Republican*, Nov. 10, 1820.

29. Mention of the subscription papers is made in the *Alabama Republican* for Aug. 3, 1821, and the address of the trustees is among the Walker Papers.

30. Incorporated Dec. 9, 1822; *Southern Advocate*, May 19, 1826.

31. *Alabama Acts*, Dec. 18, 1820; Thomas Owen, *History of Alabama*, II, 1356.

32. *Alabama Acts*, Dec. 18, 1821.

33. *House Journal, 1821*, 75 *et seq.*; *Cahawba Press*, June 29, 1822.

34. *Senate Journal, 1828*, 98.

35. *Franklin Enquirer*, Apr. 21, 1824; *Senate Journal, 1825*, 8.

36. *Ibid.*, 1828, 98.

37. *Ibid.*, 1826, 6.

38. *Ibid.*, 1827, 109-110.

39. *Senate Journal, 1828*, 13, 100, 207-208.

40. *Ibid.*, 1828, 98.

41. *Mobile Register*, Nov. 4, 1828.

42. University of Alabama, Bulletin, November, 1906.

43. In the *Minutes of the Annual Conferences, 1773-1828*, I, may be found lists of all the Alabama Methodist congregations, giving the number of members for each year beginning with 1820.

44. Royall, *Letters*, 122.

45. B. F. Riley, *History of the Baptists of Alabama*, 64; B. W. McDonnold, *History of the Cumberland Presbyterian Church*, 162-163.

46. Huntsville *Democrat*, Oct. 14, 1823; see also *Southern Advocate*, Sept. 9, 1825, July 28, 1826; Huntsville *Democrat*, Oct. 14, 1823, Oct. 27, 1826.

47. Walter C. Whitaker, *History of the Protestant Episcopal Church in Alabama*, 13. A prominent Episcopalian is quoted as saying that there may be other ways to heaven but no gentleman would take them.

48. Wyman, 118; *Mobile Register*, Apr. 29 and Nov. 4, 1828; *Franklin Enquirer*, Mar. 20, 1824.

49. Huntsville *Democrat*, May 16, 1828.

50. *Southern Advocate*, Aug. 12, 1825; *Tuscumbian*, Apr. 18, 1825.

51. Huntsville *Democrat*, Sept. 5, 1828.

52. *Mobile Register*, Jan. 1 and Feb. 28, 1828.

CHAPTER 14

1. *Southern Advocate*, Apr. 14 and Dec. 15, 1826; *Senate Journal, 1821*, 11; Birney, 55; Levasseur, II, 335-339.

2. *Senate Journal, 1825*, 12; Huntsville *Democrat*, Apr. 6, 1827,

June 30, 1826; report of a committee of the legislature appointed to investigate causes of crime, Hall Papers.

3. *Southern Advocate*, July 22, 1825.

4. Huntsville *Democrat*, June 16, 1826.

5. *Ibid.*, June 16, 1826, May 25, 1827; J. E. Saunders, *Early Settlers in Alabama*, 45.

6. Riley, *Conecuh County*, 93; Saunders, 45-46; W. E. W. Yerby, *History of Greensboro, Alabama*, 8, 12; *Tuscumbian*, Oct. 22, 1824.

7. *Ibid.*, Feb. 28, 1825.

8. Yerby, 14.

9. B. F. Riley, *Makers and Romance of Alabama History*, 584-588.

10. Royall, *Letters*, 120; *Southern Advocate*, July 8, 1825, June 1, 1827.

11. *Ibid.*, Aug. 5, 1825, July 13, 1827, Apr. 18 and 25, May 2, June 6, 1828; *Mobile Register*, July 19, 1828.

12. *Niles' Register*, XXXVI, 165.

13. *Southern Advocate*, Aug. 5, 1825.

14. Blue MS., "St. Clair County," 10; "Fayette County," 10; "Pickens County," 10.

15. Robertson, 11-13, 15-16, 36-38, 125, 139-140.

16. Huntsville *Democrat*, Apr. 12, 1825, Mar. 17, 1826, July 6 and Mar. 23, 1827; Royall, *Letters*, 95, 100.

17. Saunders, 42; Meek, *Romantic Passages*, 32-33; Blue MS., "Baldwin County," 10; "Autauga County," II, 10; "Lowndes County," 5, 10; "Wilcox County," 10; "Lawrence County," 10; "Limestone County," 10.

18. Yerby, 17-19; Royall, *Letters*, 48; A. Hodgson, *Letters*, I, 185; Huntsville *Democrat*, Apr. 13, 1827.

19. Royall, *Letters*, 46.

20. Huntsville *Democrat*, Sept. 9, 1825.

21. Birney, 42, 47-48.

22. Riley, *Baptists*, 61.

23. Saunders, 45.

24. Basil Hall, *Travels in North America in the Years 1827 and 1828*, II, 229-239.

25. Edwin C. Holland, *A Refutation of the Calumnies Circulated Against the Southern and Western States Respecting Slavery*, 48-53.

26. *The Southern Agriculturist*, II, 575-576.

27. *Alabama Republican*, Sept. 13, 1822, Aug. 29, 1823; *Alabama Journal*, Jan. 6, May 19 and Sept. 15, 1826; *Tuscumbian*, June 28, 1826; *Southern Advocate*, June 22, 1827.

28. *Alabama Acts*, Jan. 2, 1826.

29. *Ibid.*, Mar. 6, 1805.

30. *Ibid.*, Dec. 18, 1812.

31. *Southern Advocate*, Oct. 21 and June 23, 1826; Birney, 56; *Senate Journal*, 1823, 15.

32. *Alabama Acts*, Jan. 13, 1827.

33. Huntsville *Democrat*, Dec. 22, 1826.

34. Birney, 72.

35. *Ibid.*

36. *Southern Advocate*, Dec. 30, 1825. Speaking of the slave trade, the editor of this paper says: "On one vessel the slaves happily revolted and killed the crew."

37. *American Mirror*, Aug. 7, 1825.

38. *Senate Journal*, 1825, 13-14.

39. *House Journal*, 1827, 209.

CHAPTER 15

1. Henry Adams, *John Randolph* (New York, 1898), 288-289.

2. Nathaniel Macon to Bolling Hall, Feb. 13, 1820, Jan. 6, 1825, Hall Papers.

3. David Franklin Houston, *A Critical Study of Nullification in South Carolina* (New York, 1896), chap. IX; Chauncey Samuel Boucher, *The Nullification Controversy in South Carolina* (Chicago, 1916), chap. I.

4. *Mobile Register*, Nov. 28, 1826.

5. See maps at the end of Arthur Charles Cole, *The Whig Party in the South* (Gloucester, Mass., 1914).

6. *U.S. Census*, 1800, 1810, 1820.

7. Abernethy, 465.

Selected Critical Bibliography

I. MANUSCRIPT LETTERS AND PAPERS

A. B. Meek Manuscript. Alabama Department of Archives and History. These papers were assembled by Meek with the idea of publishing a history of Alabama.

A. J. Pickett Papers. Alabama Department of Archives and History. These are the unpublished papers of the author of the *History of Alabama*.

Andrew Jackson Papers. Library of Congress. This voluminous collection of letters of Jackson contains scattered information concerning Indian affairs, public lands, and politics in Alabama.

Bolling Hall Papers. Alabama Department of Archives and History. This collection of letters supplements the Bibb papers and gives an inside view of political affairs.

Charles A. Tait Papers. Alabama Department of Archives and History. These letters, copied from the originals, supplement the Bibb, Hall, and Walker papers, and are especially valuable because they contain letters from such men as William H. Crawford and John C. Calhoun, giving an insight into the political affiliations of the leaders in Alabama.

Jackson-Coffee Manuscript. Library of Congress. This collection contains about 200 letters written by Andrew Jackson to General John Coffee of Florence, Alabama, covering the kind of information mentioned in the Andrew Jackson Papers. The letters in the Library of Congress are typewritten copies of the originals.

John Williams Walker Papers. Alabama Department of Archives and History. These letters deal with the most important events in the early history of Alabama.

M. P. Blue Manuscript. Alabama Department of Archives and History. This collection, assembled by Blue, consists of information concerning the early history of several counties of Alabama contributed by various men having personal knowledge of the subject.

Mississippi Transcripts. Mississippi Department of Archives and History, Jackson. These were made by Dr. Thomas M. Owen from the original records of Mississippi Territory.

Nicholas Biddle Papers. Library of Congress. This extensive collection of letters contains instructions written by Biddle to presidents of various southern branches of the Bank of the United States. These afford some insight into the financial aspects of the cotton trade.

Thomas W. and William W. Bibb Letter Books. Alabama Dedepartment of Archives and History. This collection of letters is invaluable because of the light it throws upon relations existing between the first political leaders of Alabama and their friends in Georgia and Washington.

William L. Yancey Papers. Alabama Department of Archives and History. The collection contains the manuscript of an obituary notice of Dixon Hall Lewis which gives the best available account of the early life of that important man.

II. DOCUMENTARY MATERIAL

The published documents of the federal government, especially the *American State Papers* and the *U.S. Statutes at Large*, have been used extensively in this work. In addition, the records of the General Land Office and of the Indian Office have been searched. The local and special documents used are listed below.

Acts of the General Assembly of Alabama, 1819-1828.

Acts of the Legislature of Alabama Territory, 1819.

Aiken, John G. *Digest of the Laws of the State of Alabama,* Philadelphia, 1833.

Annals of the Congress of the United States, 1789-1825. Washington: Gales and Seaton, 1834-1856.

Brickel, R. C. *Digest of the Decisions of the Supreme Court of the State of Alabama,* Montgomery, 1874.

Hitchcock, Henry. *The Alabama Justice of the Peace,* Cahawba, 1822.

Holmes Manuscript. Executive Journal of Governor David Holmes of Mississippi Territory, 1814-1817, Mississippi Department of Archives, Jackson.

Journal of the Convention of the Alabama Territory Begun July 5, 1819. Huntsville: John Boardman, 1819.

Journal of the Council of Alabama Territory, 1818.

Journal of the House of Representatives of the State of Alabama, 1819-1828.

Journal of the Senate of the State of Alabama, 1819-1828.

Morse, Jedidiah. *Report on Indian Affairs* (1820), New Haven, 1822.

Owen, Thomas M. *Alabama Archives,* Washington, Government Printing Office, 1905.

Snedecor, V. Gayle. *A Directory of Greene County for 1855-6,* Mobile, 1856.

Tharin, W. C. *A Directory for Marengo County for 1860-61,* Mobile, 1861.

Toulmin, Harry. *A Digest of the Laws of the State of Alabama,* Cahawba, 1823.

United States House Documents, 26 Cong., 1 Sess., Doc. 172, p. 1348. Table showing condition of Alabama banks, 1819-1838.

University of Alabama. *Historical Catalogue, 1821-1870,* Tuscaloosa, 1870.

III. CONTEMPORARY SOURCES

Breckenridge, Richard. "Diary, 1816," *Alabama Historical Society Transactions,* III, 142-153, Tuscaloosa, 1898-1906. This is a good first hand account of Alabama as seen by one who came out upon the first wave of settlement.

Carter, Clarence Edwin (ed.). *The Territory of Mississippi, 1798-1817 (The Territorial Papers of the United States,* 26 vols. [Washington, 1934-]), Vol. V, Washington, 1937.

————. *The Territory of Alabama (The Territorial Papers of the United States),* Vol. XVIII, Washington, 1952.

Commons, John R., *et al.* (eds.). *A Documentary History of American Industrial Society,* Cleveland, 1910-1911. Volumes I and II, by U. B. Phillips, deal with southern agriculture, but Alabama receives little attention.

Cummins, E. H. *A Summary Geography of Alabama,* one of the United States, Philadelphia, 1819. Inaccurate, but interesting.

Darby, William. *A Geographical Description of the State of Louisiana, the Southern Part of the State of Mississippi and Territory of Alabama, with a Map,* New York, 1817.

————. *Emigrant's Guide*, New York, 1818. Contains interesting information for this early date.

Fessenden, Thomas G. *The Complete Farmer*, Philadelphia, 1839.

Gaines, George S. "Letters Relating to Events in South Alabama, 1805-1814," *Alabama Historical Society Transactions*, III, 184-192, Tuscaloosa, 1898-1906.

Garrett, William. *Reminiscences of Public Men in Alabama for Thirty Years*, Atlanta, 1872. Contains first hand information of men and events during the period under consideration.

Hall, Basil. *Travels in North America in the Years 1827 and 1828*, Philadelphia, 1829. Being a captain of the British Navy, Hall has a point of view different from that of any other traveler of that period, and his discussion of scenes in Alabama is instructive.

Hawkins, Benjamin. *A Sketch of the Creek Country, 1798-1799*, in *Collections of the Georgia Historical Society*, III, Pt. 1, Savannah, 1848. Hawkins was agent among the Creeks for many years, and this is the best available account of that Nation at the time when the pressure of the white immigration into the Southwest was beginning to tell.

Hodgson, Adam. *Letters from North America*, London, 1824. These letters, written in 1820 by a studious observer, form an important source of information.

Holland, Edwin C. *A Refutation of the Calumnies Circulated Against the Southern and Western States Respecting Slavery*, Charleston, 1822. This account of slavery is based upon conditions in South Carolina, but it is the best available Southern treatise on the subject for the period under discussion.

Levasseur, A. *Lafayette en Amerique en 1824 et 1825*, Bruxelles, 1829. The author was secretary to Lafayette during his tour of America. The account is more interesting than instructive.

Lincecum, Gideon. "Autobiography," *Publications of Mississippi Historical Society*, VIII, 443, Oxford, Miss., 1898-1914. An interesting account of the journey of one of the early immigrants to Alabama.

Macaulay, Zachary. *Negro Slavery in the United States and West Indies*, London, 1823. This gives an English view of the subject and is violently critical.

Methodist Episcopal Church. *Minutes of the Annual Conferences, 1773-1828*, Vol. I, New York, 1840. Here can be obtained statistics of the various congregations throughout the United States.

Morse, Jedidiah. *Universal Geography*, Charleston, 1819.

[Owen, John]. "John Owen's Journal of his Removal from Virginia to Alabama in 1818," *Publications of the Southern History Association*, I (April, 1897), 90-97. Another account written by an early immigrant of his journey to Alabama.

Price, T. W. *The Life of T. W. Price, Written by Himself*, Selma, 1877. There is little information of a public nature in this book.

Raymond, James. *Prize Essay on the Comparative Economy of Free and Slave Labor in Agriculture*, Frederick, Md., Frederick County Agricultural Society, 1827. This view is too superficial to be of value to the student.

Robertson, W. G. *Recollections of the Early Settlers of Montgomery County and their families*, Montgomery, 1892. This is an interesting account of an interesting community, written by one who says that "the writer was personally acquainted with every one of them."

Royall, Anne. *Southern Tours, or Second Series of the Black Book*, Washington, 1830. These letters, written on a second tour of Alabama, are interesting because they indicate the contrast produced by ten years of development in the new state.

————. *Letters from Alabama on Various Subjects, 1817-1822*, Washington, 1830. Written by an erratic woman, there is much that is personal and much that is pertinent in these letters.

Saxe-Weimar, Duke Bernhard. *Travels Through North America During the Years 1825 and 1826*, Philadelphia, 1828. Traveling the same route between New York and New Orleans that was followed by most of the foreign tourists, and passing through Montgomery and Mobile, the author gives us still another point of view.

Stuart, James. *Three Years in North America*, New York, 1833. Another and later account by one who passed along the same route followed by Saxe-Weimar and others.

Terry, Jesse. *A Portraiture of Domestic Slavery in the United States*, Philadelphia, 1817. A good Northern view.

Thwaites, Reuben Gold. *Early Western Travels*, Cleveland, 1904-1907. A large collection of accounts by travelers and explorers. The Tennessee River region is touched upon, but there is nothing for the southern part of Alabama.

Townes, S. A. *The History of Marion*, Marion, 1844. This is a good account of the establishing of a new community in Alabama.

Warden, D. B. *A Statistical, Political, and Historical Account of the United States of North America*, Edinburgh, 1819.

Welsh, Mary. "Reminiscences of Old St. Stephens," *Alabama Historical Society Transactions*, III, 208-226, Tuscaloosa,

1898-1906. This is a retrospective account by one who had known the place long since.

Woodward, Thomas S. *Reminiscences of the Creek or Muscogee Indians*, Montgomery, 1859. There is much here that does not concern Indians, and, since the author knows the ground, the information is of value.

Wyman, Justus. "A Geographical Sketch of the Alabama Territory," *Alabama Historical Society Transactions*, III, 107-127, Tuscaloosa, 1898-1906. Only a part of the original account is published here, the unpublished manuscript being in possession of the Woburn, Mass. Public Library.

IV. SPECIAL WORKS AND ARTICLES

Excepting in the case of Pickett's work and the local histories, little reliance has been placed upon secondary material dealing especially with Alabama because most of it touches but scantily upon the early period discussed in this monograph.

Abernethy, Thomas Perkins. *The South in the New Nation*, Baton Rouge, 1961.

Ball, T. H. *Clarke County, Alabama, and Its Surroundings, from 1540 to 1877*, Grove Hill, Ala. [Chicago, Press of Knight and Leonard], 1882. Contains good information of local character.

Betts, E. C. *Early History of Huntsville, Alabama*, Montgomery, 1909. This is one of the best local histories, and, because of the importance of the community, is of especial value.

Birney, William. *James G. Birney and his Times*, New York, 1890. Though only a small part of this book deals with the Alabama period of Birney's life, it contains some worthwhile information.

Blue, M. P. *History of Montgomery*, Montgomery, 1878. The author was a diligent collector of local information, and his account is of value.

———. *Churches of the City of Montgomery*, Montgomery, 1878. This account goes back to beginnings.

Brant and Fuller, Compilers. *Memorial Record of Alabama*, Madison, Wis., 1893. Too biographical; good for reference only.

Brewer, W. *Alabama: Her History, Resources, War Record, and Public Men, 1540-1872*, Montgomery, 1872. This book does

206   THE FORMATIVE PERIOD IN ALABAMA, 1815-1828

not give a good general account, but the discussion of the separate counties contains desirable information.

Brown, W. G. A History of Alabama, University, Ala., University Publishing Co., 1900. A textbook based upon insufficient material.

Burnett, E. C. "Bourbon County,"American Historical Review, XV, 66-111, 297-353.

Claiborne, J. F. H. Mississippi as a Province, Territory, and State, Jackson, 1880. This contains valuable information on the question of the division of the Mississippi Territory.

————. Life and Times of General Sam Dale, New York, 1860. A good biography of an interesting man.

Clarke, Willis G. History of Education in Alabama, Washington, 1889. Contains but little relative to the formative period.

Cobbs, Richard H., and Whittaker, Walter C. "Statistics of the Protestant Episcopal Church of Alabama," Alabama Historical Society Transactions (New Ser.), II, 83-89, Tuscaloosa, 1898-1906.

Cotterill, R. S. The Southern Indians, Norman, Okla., 1954.

Denson, John V. Slavery Laws in Alabama, Alabama Polytechnic Institute Historical Studies, Auburn, 1908.

Dewey, D. R. Financial History of the United States, New York, 1915.

Donnell, E. J. Chronological and Statistical History of Cotton, New York [published by the author], 1872. Exhaustive statistics.

DuBose, Joel C. (ed.). Notable Men of Alabama, 2 vols., Atlanta, Southern Historical Association, 1904. Little of general interest.

————. Sketches of Alabama History, Philadelphia, 1901. Contains good information on special topics.

Fenton, William N. American Indian and White Relations to 1830, Chapel Hill, 1957.

Flint, Timothy. The History and Geography of the Mississippi Valley, Cincinnati, 1833. Little information on Alabama.

Hall, J. H. B. "The History of the Cumberland Presbyterian Church in Alabama Prior to 1826," Alabama Historical Society Transactions, IV, 365-394, Tuscaloosa, 1898-1906. This gives some idea of religious conditions during the early period.

Hamilton, P. J. "Early Roads in Alabama," Alabama Historical Society Transactions, II, 39-56, Tuscaloosa, 1898-1906. Information incomplete.

————. "Some Southern Yankees," American Historical Maga-

zine and Tennessee Historical Society Quarterly, III, 303-312, Nashville, 1896-1904. Personal, but interesting.

——. "St. Stephens: Spanish Fort and American Town," *Alabama Historical Society Transactions*, III, 227-234, Tuscaloosa, 1898-1906. Not satisfying.

——. *Colonial Mobile, 1519-1821*, Mobile, 1952. A work signifying much research and containing much information.

Hammond, M. B. *The Cotton Industry*, New York, 1897. Valuable.

Hardy, John. *Selma, her Institutions and her Men*, Selma, 1879. A good local history.

Harper, Roland M. *Economic Botany of Alabama*, 2 vols., University, Ala., *Geographical Survey of Alabama*, 1913. Valuable for topographical information.

——. "A Preliminary Soil Census of Alabama and West Florida," Reprint from *Soil Science*, IV, No. 2 (August, 1917), 91-107.

Harvey, Meriwether. *Slavery in Auburn, Alabama*, Alabama Polytechnic Institute Historical Studies, Auburn, 1907. A limited view.

Haskins, Charles H. *The Yazoo Land Companies*, New York, 1891. Important for an understanding of the situation regarding the public lands.

Hodgson, Joseph. *The Cradle of the Confederacy*, Mobile, 1876. An important work, but contains little information for the early period.

Jack, Theodore H. *Sectionalism and Party Politics in Alabama, 1819-1842*, Menasha, Wis., 1919. This is the only scientific political study for this period, but little space is devoted to developments previous to Jackson's administration.

Jefferson County and Birmingham. Birmingham, 1887. (Teeple and Smith, publishers; no author given.) Too biographical to be of real service.

Johnson, Allen, and Malone, Dumas (eds.). *Dictionary of American Biography*, Vols. X, XI, New York, 1928-.

Jones, Charles C. *Antiquities of the Southern Indians*, New York, 1873.

——. *The Dead Towns of Georgia*, Savannah, 1878.

Jordan, Weymouth T. *Ante-Bellum Alabama, Town and Country*, Tallahassee, 1957.

Leftwich, George J. "Cotton Gin Port and Gaines' Trace," *Publications of Mississippi Historical Society*, VII, 263, Oxford, Miss., 1898-1914. This article throws light upon one of the earliest transportation developments in the Alabama-Mississippi region.

Little, John Buckner. *The History of Butler County, Alabama*, Cincinnati, 1885. Scant and unreliable for the early period.

Love, William A. "General Jackson's Military Road," *Publications of Mississippi Historical Society*, XI, 403-417, Oxford, Miss., 1898-1914.

McDonnold, B. W. *History of the Cumberland Presbyterian Church*, Nashville, 1888.

Malone, Henry T. *Cherokees of the Old South*, Athens, Ga., 1956.

Martin, Thomas W. *French Military Adventurers in Alabama, 1818-1828*, Birmingham, 1949.

Martin, W. E. *Internal Improvements in Alabama*, The Johns Hopkins Univ. Studs., Series 20, No. 4, Baltimore, 1902. This account is made up of undigested statistics.

Meek, A. B. *Romantic Passages in Southwestern History*, Mobile, 1857. This contains a good treatment of certain phases.

Monette, John W. *History of the Valley of the Mississippi*, New York, 1846.

Mooney, James. "Myths of the Cherokee," *Nineteenth Annual Report*, Bureau of American Ethnology, Pt. 1, 11-548.

Moore, Albert Burton. *History of Alabama and Her People*, Chicago and New York, 1927. A scholarly work; detailed and interesting.

Northern Alabama. Birmingham, 1888. (Smith and DeLand, publishers; no author given.) Scattered information of general interest, but valuable principally for biographical reference.

Owen, Thomas M. *History of Alabama and Dictionary of Alabama Biography*, 4 vols., Chicago, 1921. An encyclopedic work containing exhaustive information, and invaluable to the student of Alabama history.

Phillips, U. B. *American Negro Slavery*, New York, 1918. A most helpful treatise, covering all phases of the subject from the agricultural point of view.

———. "The Economics of the Plantation," *South Atlantic Quarterly*, II, 231. A suggestive study.

———. "The Southern Black Belt," *American Historical Review*, XI (July, 1906), 798-816. This is an interesting study of the segregation of the slave interest.

———. *The Slave Labor Problem in the Charleston District*, Boston, 1907.

———. "The Plantation as a Civilizing Factor," *Sewanee Review*, XII (July, 1906), 257-267.

————. A History of Transportation in the Eastern Cotton Belt to 1860, New York, 1908. Helpful and suggestive.

————. "Georgia and State Rights," American Historical Association Report, 1901, II, 15-224, Washington, Government Printing Office, 1902. Owing to the close relation between Georgia and Alabama politicians during the period covered by this study, this work has been of great value.

Pickett, A. J. History of Alabama, Birmingham, 1900. Though somewhat involved in details, this book represents careful research by a man who also had wide personal knowledge in his field; on many points, therefore, it is an original source. Though not without error, it is one of the few solid works covering Alabama history previous to the period of statehood.

Pitkin, Timothy. Statistical View of the Commerce of the United States, Hartford, 1816.

Powell, George. "History of Blount County," Alabama Historical Society Transactions, July 9 and 10, 1855, 31-65, Tuscaloosa, 1855. This gives valuable information for the period of early settlement.

Reeves, Jesse S. Napoleonic Exiles in America; A Study in American Diplomatic History, 1815-1819, The Johns Hopkins Univ. Studs., No. 23, 525-656, Baltimore, 1905.

Riley, B. F. History of Conecuh County, Alabama, Columbus, Ga., 1887. Gives vivid pictures of the pioneer period.

————. History of the Baptists of Alabama, Birmingham, 1895.

————. Makers and Romance of Alabama History, Birmingham, 1914. This book is made up of chapters on various unrelated topics, some of which are illuminating. Its biographical sketches are good for reference.

Riley, F. L. "Location and Boundaries of Mississippi," Publications of Mississippi Historical Society, III, 167-184, Oxford, Miss. 1898-1914.

Saunders, J. E. Early Settlers of Alabama, New Orleans, 1899. Contains good general information, and the biographical portion is sometimes useful for references.

Shackelford, Josephus. History of the Muscle Shoals Baptist Association, 1820-1890, Trinity, Ala., 1891. The point of view is so local that the work is of little value.

Shea, J. G. History of the Catholic Church in the United States, Akron, Ohio, 1890. Contains a good account of the activities of the Catholic Church in Alabama during the period under review.

Smith, Nelson F. History of Pickens County, Alabama, Carrollton, Ala., 1856. This is one of the best local histories, giving a good idea of the early development of a back county.

Somerville, H. M. "Trial of the Alabama Supreme Court Judges in 1829," in *Report of the Twenty-second Annual Meeting of the Alabama State Bar Association*, Montgomery, 1899. A good brief account.

The South in the Building of the Nation. Richmond, 1909. This is a co-operative work. The portions relating to Alabama are too general to be of value for the period under discussion.

Sparks, W. H. *The Memories of Fifty Years*, Macon, Ga., 1872. Good material for Georgia and Mississippi, but little of value for Alabama.

Stone, Alfred H. "The Cotton Factorage System of the Southern States," *American Historical Review*, XX, 557-565. This is a scientific and suggestive article.

Street, O. D. *Marshall County One Hundred Years Ago*, Guntersville, Ala., 1903. Contains some good information.

Thomas, William H. "The Birth and Growth of the Constitution of Alabama," address delivered before the Alabama State Bar Association, Montgomery, 1890. Contains some good points.

Tompkins, Alma Cole. *Charles Tait*, Alabama Polytechnic Institute Historical Studies, Auburn, 1910. A good brief account.

United States Department of Agriculture, *Atlas of American Agriculture*, Part V, Section A, Cotton, Washington, 1918. Contains valuable statistics and historical information.

Wallace, J. H. *The Alabama State Capital*, Montgomery, 1911. Contains nothing of value for the early period.

Watkins, J. L. *Production and Price of Cotton for a Hundred Years, Statistics*, U.S. Department of Agriculture Miscellaneous Bulletins, No. 9, Washington, 1895.

Weeks, Stephen B. *History of Public School Education in Alabama*, Washington, 1915. Though touching but lightly upon the early period, this is a reliable work.

West, Anson. *A History of Methodism in Alabama*, Nashville, 1893. Not a scholarly work.

Whitaker, Walter C. *History of the Protestant Episcopal Church in Alabama*, Birmingham, 1898. Contains little for the early period.

Whitfield, Gaius, Jr. "The French Grant in Alabama," *Alabama Historical Society Transactions*, IV, 321-355, Tuscaloosa, 1898-1906. This is a fairly satisfactory account of the founding of Demopolis by the Napoleonic refugees.

Williams, Thomas M. *Dixon H. Lewis*, Alabama Polytechnic Institute Historical Studies, Auburn, 1912. Considering the
available material, a satisfactory work.
Yerby, W. E. W. *History of Greensboro, Alabama*, Montgomery,
1908. Contains some useful information.

V. NEWSPAPERS AND PERIODICALS

Alabama Journal, Montgomery; Library of Congress, Dec. 9, 1825-
July 7, 1826, Nov. 28, 1828; Alabama Department of Archives,
Sept. 8, 1826-July 27, 1827.
Alabama Republican, Huntsville; Library of Congress, Jan. 5, 1819-
Apr. 22, 1825; Alabama Department of Archives, Sept. 15,
1820-Sept. 13, 1822.
Alabama Sentinel, Tuscaloosa; Library of Congress, Dec. 30, 1825.
American Farmer, Baltimore, 1820-1828.
American Mirror, Tuscaloosa; Library of Congress, Jan. 3, 1824-Feb.
26, 1825.
Cahawba Press and Alabama State Intelligencer, Cahawba; Library
of Congress, Dec. 30, 1820-July 22, 1826.
Democrat, Huntsville; Alabama Department of Archives, Oct. 14,
1823-Dec. 29, 1826.
Franklin Enquirer, Tuscumbia; Alabama Department of Archives,
Mar. 13-June 9, 1824.
Halcyon, Greensboro; Library of Congress, Apr. 24-Dec. 30, 1823.
Halcyon and Tombeckbee Public Advertiser, St. Stephens; Library
of Congress, Jan. 9-Dec. 20, 1819; Jan. 10-Nov. 27, 1820; Feb.
12-Dec. 22, 1821; Jan. 5-Nov. 2, 1822.
Kentucky Gazette, Lexington; Carnegie Library, June 13, 1814.
Mobile Argus, Library of Congress, Dec. 5, 1822-Nov. 6, 1823.
Mobile Commercial Register, Alabama Department of Archives,
Nov. 17, 1827-Dec. 5, 1828; Association Public Library, Mo-
bile, Dec. 17, 1821-Dec. 7, 1824; Dec. 9, 1825-Dec. 9, 1826;
June 4, 1828-May 29, 1829; Library of Congress, Feb. 18, 1825-
Dec. 21, 1826.
Mobile Mercantile Advertiser, Library of Congress, Dec. 18, 1824-
May 10, 1825.
Niles' Weekly Register, Baltimore, Vols. 11-36.
Republican, Savannah; Georgia Historical Society, Feb. 25 and Mar.
8, 1818.
Southern Advocate, Huntsville; Library of Congress, May 6, 1825-

Dec. 24, 1828; Alabama Department of Archives, May 6, 1825-Apr. 27 and May 18, 1827, and following.

The Southern Agriculturist, Charleston, Vols. 1 and 2, 1828-1829.

Tuscumbian, Tuscumbia; Alabama Department of Archives, Sept. 1, 1824-Jan. 17, 1827.

Washington Republican, Washington, Mississippi Territory; Mississippi Department of Archives, Apr. 13, 1813-Dec. 27, 1817.

Index